# THE E FACTOR

## ENTREPRENEURIAL COMPETENCIES FOR PERSONAL AND BUSINESS SUCCESS

We work with leading authors to develop the strongest educational materials bringing cutting-edge thinking and best learning practice to a global market.

Under a range of well-known imprints, including Financial Times/Prentice Hall, Addison Wesley and Longman, we craft high quality print and electronic publications which help readers to understand and apply their content, whether studying or at work.

Pearson Custom Publishing enables our customers to access a wide and expanding range of market-leading content from world-renowned authors and develop their own tailor-made book. You choose the content that meets your needs and Pearson Custom Publishing produces a high-quality printed book.

To find out more about custom publishing, visit www.pearsoncustom.co.uk

# THE E FACTOR

## ENTREPRENEURIAL COMPETENCIES FOR PERSONAL AND BUSINESS SUCCESS

### by DAVID GIBSON

PEARSON
Custom
Publishing

Pearson Education Limited
Edinburgh Gate
Harlow
Essex CM20 2JE

And associated companies throughout the world

*Visit us on the World Wide Web* at:
www.pearsoned.co.uk

First published 2006

This Custom Book Edition © 2006 Published by Pearson Education Limited

ISBN-13  978 1 84479 583 3
ISBN-10  1 84479 583 7

Printed and bound in Great Britain by Antony Rowe Limited

# CONTENTS

# PREFACE

Welcome to my world. The world of the Entrepreneur. I spend most of my waking time, lecturing, researching and advising Entrepreneurs. Heck I may even be an Entrepreneur myself as I have started and ran all sorts of businesses, full and part time, though admittedly with a mixed degree of success. What I do love doing most of all is learning how anyone performs to their best ability and passing these lessons on.

Everywhere you go nowadays you are encouraged to be "more enterprising or more innovative" Every billboard screams at you to "go for it!". For what?

The basic message seems to be that we all should become Entrepreneurs, start businesses and live happily ever after. Some of you will want to start your own business; and some of you should never be allowed near a business. Others will have no desire to go into business but want to make a different to their local community or to help their family or friends to achieve their potential.

I believe that anyone can benefit from learning the skills or competencies that make a good Entrepreneur. Good Entrepreneurs spend their working life dealing with change, spotting opportunities and making things happen. I don't know whether any of you work in the voluntary sector or in a company, but you will notice that change is the name of the game. Technology, world events and other factors combine to move the pace of change onwards at an ever increasing rate.

An Entrepreneur can cope with this, because he/she sees change as an opportunity to innovate to survive and grow. We all need to adopt this mindset whatever our ambitions or interests in life. For those of you already working as an Entrepreneur, you will know that most training or books focus on giving you useful knowledge about

Business and leaving you to it. My contention is that you need to develop your "efactor", that is work on key traits/habits which give you the best possible chance of dealing with change and being the best you can be.

I feel I have discovered a core set of competencies which most Entrepreneurs have or need to perform to their potential. Of course there are exceptions. Sometimes you get someone who does almost everything wrong, but because of a strong competitive advantage in the market place or some other key variable they manage to make significant profits, at least in the short term.

I have two points I would like to make regarding this. Firstly improvement in their "e competencies" would be more likely to sustain rather than threaten any success they have had to date. Secondly my definition of Entrepreneur is not restricted to someone who has made several million and has a Bentley, but rather anyone who identifies a need/ opportunity, and take action to make that project happen, whether for profit or not. I believe that anyone could benefit by improving their "e factor". It is the key to personal excellence, an outcome we should all aim for to improve the quality of our own and the lives of those around us.

Read this book but more importantly practice using the ideas in your everyday life. As a friend once said to me "use it, just don't read about it; otherwise what is the point"?

I would love to tell you that reading this book will change your life but my street wisdom dictates that I tell you the truth. Read, the book.; practice the ideas in real life; bounce back when they don't always work the first time you try them; keep learning and practising, and then my son/daughter you will be good!

Go for it!! And have the good luck all us Entrepreneurs need !!

Regards
David Gibson

---|---

# INNOVATION AND CREATIVITY

The key skill any Entrepreneur has is the ability to spot opportunities to find markets and to find innovations to solve problems.

In this era of rapid technological change the ability to find innovative solutions is a key requirement whether you are in business or not. It is not just enough to come up with a new idea for a product or project.

In making the project happen you will continue to have unforeseen problems. Can you continue to adapt and innovate to move the project forward whatever the difficulty?

Organisations which have followed the same methods of operation for a number of years in the past, now have to "go with the flow" and adapt to the rate of change.

So are you good at coming up with new ideas or do you find it difficult? It doesn't matter you can improve your creativity. It is a skill like anything else which needs practice.

Lets do a little test. Have any of you ever written a poem, a song or appeared in a play? Have you ever drawn a picture?

I defy any of you to say you have never done any of these activities. As a child you are encouraged to use your imagination, play games and have fun. Once you reach the ages of 11/12 the education systems tends to focus on developing your logical and analytical thinking. Unless you excel at art or music there is little room in the curriculum for coming up with new ways to tackle things.

When I teach Creativity I like to set the class a problem usually involving coming up with new product services to solve problems. For instance the task might read "in groups outline 5 problems young people between 18-30 have and devise 2 new products/services to solve these".

Some of the students really struggle initially. They are not attuned to using creativity, gradually however they start having fun, having silly ideas and start finding innovative solutions all over the place. The group dynamic helps, but also gradually the students start to get a belief that they could make a difference. When you realise, you could come up with an idea which could make a difference, you start to look at ways of being enterprising and making the idea happen.

It is amazing the change of attitude. The problem always with training/teaching is this, people forget to take the simple steps which can make the difference between applying their thoughts and turning knowledge into action. I usually get the students to sign an agreement to do 3 things and I want you to do the same now.

If you keep to this agreement for 30 days you are increasing your chance of being more innovative.

## INNOVATION

Agreement

I _____ do hereby agree to

1. Be more curious and look for unusual connections.  I promise to do a few things differently from normal each week
2. I promise to buy a small notebook, take it everywhere for 30 days and write at least one new idea every day
3. Every time I face a problem for the next thirty days I will ask myself the following questions:

What can I learn from this?

What can I do to turn this around?

I promise to challenge normal solutions and not make assumptions about people or situations.

Signed _____

Date _____

   Please confirm to me by e-mail as to whether you have kept your part of your agreement.  If you haven't please do not read anymore. This book is for doers!

## INNOVATION AND IDEAS

### Task

(a)   name 5 problems young people ages 18-30 have

(b)   find two new products and two new services which might solve one of these problems

(c)   which is your best idea?

If possible do this with 2 friends.

### Review

Part of being innovative is an attitude of mind.  Do you believe you can find new ways to do things?  I hope you realise you can.  It is simply being open to possibilities.

Look at some of the role models.  I came across the story of a lady who found her son had ran up a £500 monthly phone bill about six months ago.  She worked in a video shop and was not a scientist. She did however have a problem and was not sensible enough to realise she was too stupid to solve it.  She came up with a rough design of a box unit which would block out certain numbers so that her son could not ring them.

It was simple but six months later it is available for sale at £30 in every B&Q in UK and the lady is set to have a substantial success – What was so special about what she did?

She had a problem and she tried to solve it.  She used simple technology and her solution was basic.  However everyone who has a teenage son or daughter are warned about screening calls/websites etc that their children might come across.  Everyone will want to buy a unit.

Again it is not just the concept that a great idea could make you or your organisation a lot of money it is the contribution that it can make – for instance if you came up with a product or service that could benefit the community and donate it to a charity who can either raise money from it or use it to solve problems of their target group that is equally enterprising. Basically in Business or life, people have been trying to find new solutions to challenges. To make a difference you need to be prepared to think differently. Adopt a "what if" mindset.

So get going! One idea a day from now on.

## Case Study

Lets look at a live case study. I'm sitting writing this chapter on a Sunday afternoon in May. Behind me my teenage son is sitting at the computer. He is not interested in School – He is 15 and shows very little motivation. My wife and I try to explain to him how you should work harder at school if he wants to have a good career.

I don't think we are getting through and neither are his teachers.

The easy answer is to give up, let him learn his own lessons. However I am the person telling you to come up with Innovative ideas so let look at solutions "outside the box".

How can I bring it across to him the consequences of no work and no qualifications? Is there a film he can watch? Is there a teenage tv programme which puts across this lesson? Who are his role models? What about a song or book or TV programme that tells their story but puts across the points:

1. qualifications can open doors
2. work hard – if you want to achieve something

How can I use texting, the internet, TV his Ipod any of the medium he uses to get information?

The traditional answer locally is to get him to go to Church, join the boy scouts and do the Duke of Edinburgh Award, all of which he rejects. If he does not respond to that stereotype what else can I do?

He has some interest in Business or Drama, how can I bring this alive so he can see what life would be like in these areas. How about inventing a game? Put it on computer? How about a virtual reality business experience? How about setting up a competition? Use texting etc to stay in touch. How about a business thriller written by a teenager? How about a play which he acts in which is based in a teenager starting a business? You can see the ideas are starting to flow. I will keep you posted. If I can solve the problem I reckon a lot of parents throughout the world would love to know my solution.

So watch this space. Maybe I should share the profits with you!!

### Is It a Process or Not?

There is a lot of argument as to whether you can follow a strict procedure to get creative ideas or whether this goes against the whole idea of creativity, making random connections and "thinking outside the box".

I think again it would be rigid to exclude any method. You have to experiment to see what works for you. The most important thing is output, ideas that make a difference.

As mentioned earlier being curious, doing things differently and having a notebook to record random thoughts is a good start and is simple (buy a little notebook today. Carry it with you everywhere, and I mean everywhere).

It would be remiss not to discuss the work of the inventor of "lateral thinking". Edward De Bono. He believes that creativity is a process which can be taught at any level. He believes in the concept of provocation, which is to challenge the traditional assumptions in any situation if you join an organisation you are capable of spotting very quickly things that happen "because that is the way we always do it".

He believes that creativity is vital as all organisations need to challenge themselves and be proactive in seeking improvement.

De Bono devised a model "the six thinking hats" which encourages individuals to look at problems wearing different hats representing different problems.

The key to this is focus. If you have a problem focus on it and solutions will come from the most unusual sources, partly because your subconscious is ticking away thinking of connections whilst you might be doing something like sleeping or watching TV. This may lead to your "eureka" moment like Archimedes in the bath. I have found some of my best ideas whilst out running.

## Innovation

De Bono comes up with various strategies to look at the problem from the outside. Another interesting strategy developed in Russia from the study of major discoveries is the use of a number of terms and processes and applying the problem. One example would be the use of "reverse" where you do the complete opposite of everything that has been done to date, as a model of change.

## The Disney Model

Another popular model is "The Disney Model" of creativity specifically modelling the techniques devised by Walt Disney. You basically be as creative as possible, suggest any number of solutions. Then you criticise and try to pull them apart. You eventually try to pick the ideas that work best for you that are creative but also have business sense.

As you can imagine "The Disney Model" has a big focus on letting your imagination run riot to create lots of unusual possibilities and to make connections between two contrasting areas and looking for the common ground.

## Attitude and Mind

It is important to have clearly defined goals and problems. What is it you want to sort out?

It is also important to diagnose them and to have good core belief like "there is always a way to sort things out". Otherwise people or companies get too emotional about a problem, visualise the worst possible consequences and tend to "freeze" like a rabbit in headlights even though the solution is obvious to a detached outsider.

You need to focus on times and situations when you have come up with a solution to what seemed an impossible problem.

Try to find someone to model who is notorious for solving problems in an innovative way. Take a problem to them. Watch what they do, how they react what processes they go through. You will probably find that they are relaxed, and have a belief that they will solve the problem and will have access to some good resources and lateral thinkers. Anyway to get a model watch what they do. Copy them and you will find you will get a degree of their success.

## Groups

There is no set rule that you must work in groups. However what other people do provide is a different perspective to your own. The ideal group suitable for "brainstorming" an idea are people with a diverse group of experience. If you are a group of say six twenty five year old accountants I am not saying that you all think exactly the same but you are unlikely to bring enough of a mix to solve a problem which is proving too challenging for logical analytical thinkers represented by Accountants and Lawyers.

My idea would be to create your own group of friends, co workers who are as different as possible from each other, who meet on a regular basis to come up with new ideas/innovations. I first came across this idea when I was taking a women's Enterprise programme.

All of the participants on the programme had a business idea and the ladies all came from different backgrounds. There were lawyers, accountants, artists, housewives and teachers. We then took the idea of one of the participants and "brainstormed". The ideas and the innovation to the ideas flowed and every participant was left with much improved ideas, alternative markets and methods of operation. Why did it happen? First of all there is a group dynamic where everyone seemed to perform better as a team. The group had been given some time to gel and there were no major conflicts. However the key to the success was the fact that everyone had different perspectives on the problem. The artist was able to help the lawyer and vice versa. This is a key to Innovation. Everyone has a different perspective and something to offer if you are prepared to give them time and effort to make their contribution. It was amazing how the housewife could give the computer science a perspective on how families and children use PC's and what were the important benefits to look for.

You may well work as part of a team or have a group of friends who hang around together. If the group is comfortable together that alone is a good start.

However also consider forming a specific innovation group" with a range of people with diverse skills and background all who have a common aim to produce ideas with commercial application.
Key features that will ensure the group success will be:

1.  the building of group rapport
2.  someone to lead and motivate the team
3.  a process which the group likes to practice new ideas
4.  some form of motivation for the best idea
5.  someone in charge of follow up/implementation of an idea

It may take some time to find the right group of people but it can pay dividends – ideally you need the normal mix to make a team successful.

The person who can think laterally, the person who can share, the person who perceives the problems and the facilitator.

There is no rule which says that groups will come up with better ideas than individuals but try it out, get the right group dynamic and watch those ideas flow.

**Tony Buzan**

Tony Buzan the inventor of mindmaps is another person who offers ideas and solutions to boost your creativity.

His focus is on thinking and the brain. He has however some surprisingly simple applications that you could apply to boost your creativity.

1. Take breaks: I thought you might like this one!!
2. Go for long walks
3. Be creative in your everyday life. He believes you can bring creativity into relationships, cooking and setting a table for instance
4. Create your own imaginary mastermind group – a little weird perhaps. Select people who you admire as resourceful and creative. They could be business people or politicians or even historical characters. When you have got a problem ask them what you should do!! I rather like this idea and as I am sharing it with you I promise to do this for the next ninety days and then put an honest report on the E factor website.
5. Use Buzan's mind mapping process. This is a diagrammatic way of putting all your knowledge on an area in diagrammatic fashion.

Let me do one for you for the E Factor starting with the title in the centre and show a plan of the book. Here goes!!

**Figure 1–1**

**E FACTOR**

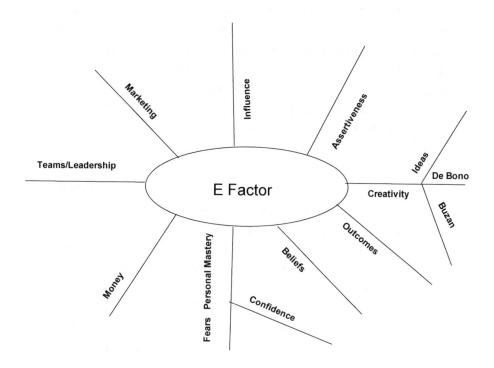

It is simply a way of arranging your creative thoughts.

Buzan does suggest you dance, sing, play music and draw.

He believes in:

1. seeing things from different viewpoints
2. make combinations

He also believes as we have suggested already that you should be curious like a child.

## Conclusion

I am not saying that either Buzan or De Bono have it sussed. It is important to practice being creative and if a structure helps you to do this well and good. If not do it anyway, find what stimulates you. You may be like Archimedes and find the bath is the best place. The important thing is to have the idea. Equally important is doing something with the idea. There are no marks for bright ideas that are not acted upon. That is another essential ingredient of the Entrepreneur the ability to take action and we will look at that later!!

So let us try and summarise what we have learned.

Yes you are a creative powerhouse. Your only problem is that you do not realise it yet. It is a life skill from which anyone can benefit. Like all competencies some of you will already have the skill at unconscious competence level already. That is you are creative without thinking about it and are recognised as a very resourceful person because you always came up with an innovative solution to any problem. However if you have spent twenty years becoming an Engineer practising analytical thinking you have some work to do to use creativity in your everyday life. I hasten to add that no one is saying you need to abandon all logic just add creativity to your thinking skills to get the best results.

## The Creativity Test

Have you ever come up with a new idea? Have you ever imagined the future? Have you ever done things differently? Have you ever solved a problem you were thinking about earlier as you drove along in the car? If so you have been creative. Have you ever challenged an assumption about the way things are normally done? You have been innovative.

It is important that you believe you can come up with new ways of doing things. It is honestly half the battle. You are relaxed you expect to find a solution and because of this expectation, surprise you do.

## Make a Commitment

Make a commitment now that for the next ninety days you will practice being creative and looking for innovation.

## Be Curious and Dare to Fail

There are all sorts of people, circumstances and opportunities surrounding us every day. We all expect that we have got to maybe go to USA or the Far East to find some new innovation. The truth is, a new innovation may be right in front of you. I don't know if you have ever heard the parable "acres of diamonds" where a man leaves home and spends his whole life searching for diamonds and dies in poverty without finding any. After his death, diamonds are found on his own ground. The moral of the story is look around you and you will find your own acre of diamonds right in your own life circumstances or contacts. Be prepared to be open and to look at opportunities that may not amount to anything. As the founder of IBM said "be prepared to fail more" you will come up with some crazy ideas and some good ideas that will lack a key ingredient that will mean it will be consigned to the cutting room floor.

The key thing about creativity is that if you will make it part of your everyday life, you will have a consistent stream of ideas and will not be tied to the one good idea you have had by chance.

## Dare To be Different

The chances are that any innovation is likely to be something new and uncertain. As something new it will meet opposition as many people and organisations whatever their public profile do not like change.

Many of us (even those who write books about creativity and enterprise!!) are creatures of habit. I find myself enjoying little routines. I like to set off for work at the same time, go the same route to the office, listen to the same radio show, park in the same space, go to the same café for breakfast and read the same newspaper. Bore of the year or what??

So I fight this. Some days I will go a different route, I will read a completely different paper – I will change everything. Why? The danger is if you keep doing the same things the same way all of the time you will keep getting the same results.

That is why certain innovation experts such as Dr John Park of Robert Gordon University in Aberdeen worry about too rigid processes/structures in coming up with ideas. The worry is that you will limit your range of innovative solutions, because you are again sticking too rigidly to a routine.

So go out of your way to have new experiences, travel to new places to get the stimulation you need. To innovate you are constantly looking for associations or connections between products, people and markets that have no obvious link. For instance mobile phones tend to be mainly the preserve of the young, with teenagers being particularly adapt at using all the features such as texting, ringtones. Elderly people (not all) are as a group not as happy with new technology, many don't own mobile phones and shy away from using them too much.

However recently with a group of 300 nurses when explaining new ideas we explored the Health and Social Problems of the elderly. The nurses identified many different problems including their difficulty in communication with the outside world and inability to use the simplest technology which would help significantly with safety, health and other personal and social issues. When the group brainstormed, they came up with a new mobile phone with a few basic keys for an old person to press, less of a toy more a simple device that would meet the needs of the elderly for instant communication.

Just to show that great minds think alike 02 announced a week later in the press that they were designing such a product.

**Set Yourself a Daily Creativity Goal**

Buy yourself a small notebook and write one new idea in it every day. Carry it everywhere.

The point I am trying to get across is that idea generation is not something you do to find a new project or a solution. It is something you should continually do and you will find you will have to continually innovate as a project is implemented.

*Daydream*

Like me you may have been told off many times not to daydream. However using your imagination, visualising situations and unusual connections is a great way to stimulate creativity. Einstein arrived at his famous theory of relativity whilst imagining travelling on a time machine back and forward in timelines. A proven technique that you may want to try is when you have got a goal or challenge is to visualise yourself having achieved the end result and then work back to see what stages you have gone through to get that end result. Again you have "fooled" your mind that you have arrived at the end result and your subconscious will not recognise the difference and is likely to show the pathway to the end result something that a logical planning process will have difficulty arriving at.

**Competitive Advantage**

Again unless you are lucky enough to be setting up a business or to work for an organisation that has unlimited resources you need innovation as your competitive advantage to compete with the "big boys". You may not have the money to devise a traditional marketing strategy but instead will have to adapt "guerrilla" strategies, marketing plans that can help you reach the customer without traditional advertising and expenditure.

## So Where do Ideas Come From?

Ideas can come from anywhere. You can find an idea simply by listening respectfully to anyone. As far as I am concerned one of the most innovative businesses of recent years was "The Big Issue". The owner listened to the need for many people trying to re-establish themselves on the work ladder to earn money independently and funded a very successful business which also is a strong social enterprise.

## Market Trends

The press and market reports will let you know major trends. What are the trends of today? A vastly increased aging population; the power of the mobile phone as a communications tool; the opening up of international trade borders; the economic growth of China and India; the list is endless. There are unlimited ideas from these trends alone.

## A Personal Problem

What really pisses you off? Chances are it pisses a lot of other people off too. Solve it and you have a potential idea.

## Technology

Innovation is much more about an attitude of mind which you must bring to your future work/life pursuits. However technology is developing at such a fast rate. However, it can speed most processes up. It can add value in many cases. It is not always the answer. Technological products can take ten years to devise, but maybe the simple use of basic technology to solve a problem can make a significant impact.

## Different Industries

Businesses and social organisations operate differently. How an airplane manufacturer markets his product will be very different from how financial services are marketed. How staff are treated in universities may differ significantly from how staff in a manufacturing plant are handled, and so on. What would happen if you transferred some of the learning strategies from one industry to another? In some cases it could transform an industry's results. For instance lawyers tend to adopt a fairly narrow range of marketing strategies, many relying on reputations and long standing professional relationships. What about if you were a newly formed practice how would you establish market share? How about looking at how companies operate in intensely competitive sales environments. ? If you took the strategies, customised them and ensured there was nothing against professional guidelines, your innovation could make a substantial and lasting impact.

## Association Connection Searching

As discussed, it is the new connections between different areas that can produce the innovation. You need to constantly search for these.

De Bono, Buzan and many of the other creativity gurus all have created tools to stimulate connection making. For instance there is a random word game which encourages you to take three words build crazy connections and then take the ideas from there.

Let us do this and take three random words that occur to me now. McDonalds (I am writing this in a branch of the great "healthfood chain!!) Pets (I was thinking of my cat, sad I know) Enterprise (I spend my life encouraging and people to be more enterprising and helping business and organisation be more entrepreneurial and create results).

Here we go –

1.  "McDonalds" for pets
2.  A pet franchise organisation
3.  Place to keep pets outside any food store
4.  Promotion scheme for McDonalds to provide money for pet sanctuaries
5.  Any pet franchises as businesses – grooming, psychology, pet hotels etc.
6.  Establish pet products with a new brand name
7.  Creativity classes for pet owners
8.  Pet characters?? For enterprise ???
9.  Use animal skills behaviours as a way of teaching people to be enterprising
10. Marketing links between pet skills and McDonalds
11. A social enterprise to promote worldwide pet club promoted through McDonalds
12. Use the McDonalds child friendly marketing strategies to market pets to dogs
13. Learn business skills through pet handling
14. Pure vegetarian McDonalds!!
15. McDonalds staff training – Customers as pets
16. Pet service units set up to be as efficient as a McDonalds
17. Pet as new children's character to replace Ronald McDonald
18. Pet walking, cleaning product of business and enterprise training
19. Pet products for school enterprise projects
20. McDonalds pet food shops

Some very wacky ideas.  I know but I just wanted to illustrate the process openly and honestly.

There are plenty of completely useless ideas but some connections to take forward.  Watch out for the new pet McDonalds character coming to a store near you. A week later I have just spotted a success book based on sheepdog strategies. Weird or what?

You are likely to achieve the best results if you practice creativity on an ongoing basis, if you get other people involved who can provide different perspectives and market knowledge, and where you are motivated to solve a particular problem.

Without taking time and practice you will not improve this significant E Factor. It is only half of the equation for the enterprising person. There are many great ideas people who are not necessarily successful business people. However the creation of a new idea can transform lives, and not only that of the idea generator. Life is a constant challenge, identifying solutions which provide significant commercial or community opportunity is a worthwhile contribution. Make sure you do your bit.

### What Makes A Good Idea?

Hopefully now you are a creativity powerhouse bursting with ideas (well at least you have one idea which you hope might work).

How do you know whether it is a good idea or not?

I feel a good idea will have a clear market, will make some use of technology, will ideally have some international potential and be capable of being protected. It also makes life easier if you do not require years of research or huge finance although on a cost benefit analysis produced the long term market may suggest the idea is feasible.

It depends what you want from your idea or creative thought; you may simply only want to deal with the challenge your local Help the Aged store faces and have no interest in making a more significant contribution. However my argument is that as an Enterprising person your wish to have wider impact can lead to greater financial reward or contribution for either you, the business you work for, community organisation or charity you nominate to benefit for your innovation.

Your idea might be the greatest technical innovation ever, but if no one wants it, it is likely to disappear without a trace.

If your idea can be copied and you can't protect your ownership of it you are likely to lose it. Some ideas are "me too" and because they lack innovative content you will lose any competitive advantage unless you build some new way of doing things into the venture. Sadly some good ideas will also be stolen. A new invention with market potential is worth a significant sum of money and you need to contact the patent office as soon as possible to see if you can protect it.

The good news is that if you can, and it has market potential there are likely to be some help from outside bodies to pay part of the cost of protection.

Trademarks, logos, designs and copyright also all provide some form of cover. Perhaps one of the easiest is to get anyone you talk to, to design a non disclosure agreement before you discuss it in detail.

Having once taught a female participant on an Enterprise course for three months without ever knowing her idea, and therefore finding it hard to help develop it. I do sometimes find people to be overly secretive but there is no use denying it, there are some sharks out there. Ask Dyson of Vacuum cleaner fame who spent ten years fighting to protect his patent. It would be unfair to make you think that once you have the patent no one will trouble you. There are plenty of major contributories who will test your capacity and finances for a long legal fight. The realities are that the involvement of a University company or major sponsor can help with the protection.

The other reality is that getting to market as quickly as possible is almost your greatest protection of the Intellectual Property.

## Commercial Help

It is important that once you have generated a new idea which you want to implement that you do some assessment work. The first thing is to assess the resources to make it happen. Have you got access to money market intelligence networking and prototype and produced development help? Who can provide it? You will find regional development agencies very helpful here. Not only have they got staff and resources to help but they are constantly searching to promote "Global businesses" Any product or service with international potential becomes a possible economic contribution to the region.

You also need to self assess. Have you got some commercial skills? Can you make it happen, and are you willing to develop yourself along with the product? Some business people like Sir Alan Sugar for instance seemed to have creative capacity and the ability to make things happened and to influence to get results.

There are others particularly those within academic and technical functions who can develop the idea, but are very deficient in any of the other E Factor Skills. The whole message of this book is that you can develop your competencies in all these areas. However although significant development is possible if you are willing to learn and apply or if you are very creative but lack many of the other qualities, it can be sound business practice to either bring other Entrepreneurs into the team or in some cases to consider protecting your intellectual property to licence others to use it. If need be, enlist the help of independent advisers to assess the best options. However what I do believe is that whatever you prefer to do, create or implement you should work on the other half of the equation even only to appreciate what is being done.

If not the Innovators may change the product you make, or the business people may attempt to "wipe your eye". If in doubt read "the streetwise guide to starting your own business" to learn some of the business realities, if only to make decisions and ask the right questions.

## If You Work Somewhere Who Owns The Idea?

If you are working for a company and you develop an innovation be very clear who owns the rights. If in doubt get independent advice. Many of the most recent innovative contributors do not necessarily end up with financial reward for their innovations and many don't care. However go into it with your eyes open.

The inventor of the Internet, one of the most significant innovations in recent years has not achieved financial reward. There is nothing wrong with this; it depends on your motivation. Just make sure you get what you want as Intellectual property can be very valuable.

### Be Innovative Or Die!!

A bit of a dramatic statement but long gone are the days where individual companies and the public sector could afford to "rest on their laurels". There is constant change, global competition and continuous technological development. If an organisation or an individual does not respond to this they are likely to be left behind.

Innovation is an attitude of mind. Even when you have a good product or service you need to focus your attention on certain types of questions. Does this product or service need to change to meet client needs? How can I improve my contribution to the client? What do we need to do now to take this forward?

Depending on our business or job, we are not always allowed to use the wanton experimentations which can provide useful feedback.

If you are a Doctor for instance, you must follow certain procedures to ensure the medical health and safety of your patient. However that does not mean that you should not be open to new ideas or to problems that your patients have that are not met. You also if you want to lead, should be looking to find new ways to help staff use resources and ensure you and your colleagues are the best you can be.

### Am I Expected To Be Creative?

Obviously if you are starting a new business you will be searching for a new idea and be forced to be innovative to survive as conditions and markets constantly change. However those of you going into professions will find that you are expected to innovate and contribute creatively.  Professions and their professional bodies demand you have to adapt to ongoing change.

## Can I Do It?

I have tried to tell you constantly that you can do it.  The first precondition is that you should want to do it and be convinced that you must otherwise you will self sabotage.  Secondly you must practice it in real life.  I am about to set you a task which I want you to complete and return to me by email within the next thirty days.

Why I am doing this.  It is because I passionately believe there is a strong difference between knowing what to do and actually doing it. You need creativity and innovation to become for you a competency something like driving which most of you probably do now without any conscious thought.  To reach there you are going to have to go through stages of practicing it, getting it wrong, getting sabotaged by others, get to the stage of making good progress by persisting and finally doing it as part of your range of behaviours.  It will take persistence, commitment and the willingness to learn but above all it will take action.

It is up to you to decide are you happy to be aware of the growing importance of creativity and innovation or do you want to use some of it to be more enterprising and improve some aspect of your work life situations?

As always it is up to you.  If I was your personal coach I would be there to motivate you and cajole you everyday.  If you need this help find someone who is prepared to help you.

Although this book contains eight separate E Factors.  I believe that creativity is amongst the most important as I believe identifying opportunities and then making them happen are the key enterprise qualities that not only any budding entrepreneur should have, but also anyone who wants to be personally excellent in whatever their choice of career or community volunteering.

I promise you not only will you perform better in work/enterprise but the same qualities can also improve your personal/family life.

How can you be more innovative in your relationships with children, friends, family or partner?

NOW. It is time to complete the task. You are not allowed to move onto the next chapter, unless you email me with the task. I'm watching you!!

## INNOVATION AND CREATIVITY

### The Task

A large American Multinational has recruited you as its "Innovation Trainee" on £50,000 per annum. You have been set the following tasks and must provide a short 500 word report to the managing director with your answers

Tasks

1.  (a) Identify ten problems/challenges that teenagers have
    (b) Come up with five new products and five services that will help them
    (c) Pick your best idea and explain your reasons
    (d) Outline the first four things you would do to take your idea forward
    (e) Explain what you will do everyday o become a more creative person

(500 words)

Email – Efactor@aol.com

# ──── 2 ────

# **PERSONAL MASTERY**

## **PERSONAL MASTERY**

### **Introduction**

Really starting your own business or developing a successful corporate or community enterprise should be straightforward. You read a "how to" manual (like the streetwise guide to starting your own business), you achieve your goals, become rich and famous and live happily ever after. Yet it rarely happens, because possibly your biggest problem will be yourself. We all know what we should do and yet we don't do it.

### **Why?**

We all have difficulty in taking action and doing the right thing. The ability to control our emotions and win the "inner game" with ourselves is very important. We all have a psychological make up and have been programmed by our life experience to date. Your performance in your career or business or life in general depends on your beliefs, focus, self esteem, confidence and ability to control your emotions. The question is whether you can change your make up or indeed whether you want to. The problem is that you may hold yourself back from being the best you can be.

We are however creatures of habit. If you have been programmed by life experiences and your family over the past twenty years "you lack confidence" you are useless at anything practical. You tend to have very engrained habits and you tend to believe what you are told. The longer this goes on (those of you who like the author are over 35 pay attention!) the more challenging it will be to break free from that mindset. It is a bit like going under in a swimming pool, you will have to make a tremendous effort to escape your part programming.

## Can You Change?

Of course you can. People change habits all the time. They get into a different environment or get some reason strong enough to get them to act differently. Have you ever met a bride to be who had not slimmed before her "big day"? I have met several men with chronic smoking and exercise habits. After a stroke when it is spelt out to them their life prognosis if they don't change their habits, there was a remarkable change.

It is a pity though that it has to be a life or death experience (I don't mean the marriage) to get us to change. What you have to do is use some of the principles in these cases to help bring about the change. However you have to want to change. Other people may suggest the changes as good strategy but you have to want it yourself.

Also research has shown it is easier to make big changes in your outlook or beliefs a which can lead on to several smaller changes.

## Beliefs/Values

Your beliefs play a fundamental part in your success/performance. If you start a new project where there is a degree of uncertainty there are plenty of people who will forecast its failure, simply because of the fact it is new and untested. You need to have a strong belief in yourself and your project. This is a key selling point for any potential suppliers/customers/investors.

I come from Northern Ireland where people are natural pessimists. There is nothing wrong with some degree of realism or preparation against unexpected events. However you will need strong belief if you are to keep going when you meet the inevitable setbacks. The power of belief in business and support is illustrated in the recent survival of West Bromich Albion in the Premiership football league. In the thirteen years since its existence the team that was bottom of the league by Christmas were always relegated. In this season 2004/5 the team was West Brom led by their new manager Bryan Robson a great ex footballer with an indifferent managerial career and no wins in his first twelve league matches. Somehow he managed to instil a belief in the team that they could survive and break all the unwritten rules.

## What Are Your Beliefs?

List three beliefs you have about life in general. List 3 beliefs you have about your own ability and three you have about business.

Analyse them, are they all positive beliefs that give you confidence and hope in everything you do.? Or are there some negative beliefs in there some uncertainty which may undermine all your efforts.

I came across one client who had experienced business failure in the past. After years of relative success he got involved in a get rich quick venture which was doomed to failure. He was almost "brain-washed" into believing the project would work by other associates and it failed through no fault of his own.

Samuel had always succeeded in life where he had put in hard work either as a child or adult. This affected him badly.

He eventually started a new business taking business seminars as he had a talent for presentation – However every time he recruited for a course when things started to go wrong he literally gave up. It was almost as if he was looking for the excuse to bolster his new belief "nothing ever works". This was ironic because as part of his day time job, Samuel was involved in recruiting participants for programmes and was always successful. Obviously this situation required urgent attention. Let me tell you some of the things we did to challenge this.

## Challenge the Beliefs

I spend some time with Samuel talking over the three recruitment drives for courses where he had quit. On each occasion when something went wrong "I just felt it wasn't going to work out". I started to test his belief "Have you ever ran a successful course?" yes he had "What would happen if you kept going whatever the problems?" "I might fail" "Would that be so bad?" "no" Just because one business venture failed, does that mean you will, always be a failure?" "my wife thinks so" "What do you think?" "I don't know" – "What if I said you get £5,000 if you could show me you gave everything to recruiting the course whatever the result?" He smiled, "I guess I would really go for it" Why don't you take this attitude?

### Visualisation

I asked him to visualise the course recruitment being successful and finding it easy to get new participants and working out as a great success.

I told him to do it twice a day for five minutes. I wanted him to do this for thirty days. He did as he was asked and I believe this was a factor in boosting his belief and ability to take action. Your sub-conscious mind responds to images, sounds and feelings. If you continually visualise your outcome you go a long way towards convincing yourself that it will actually happen. It's something that sports people do as part of their training routine.

### Get a Set of Empowering Beliefs

No one can confirm whether a belief is true or not. People do some-times have very strong self delusional beliefs which can lead to irrational actions. For instance there are a lot of different fundamental, religious beliefs about where the "believers" feel they must impose the death penalty on non believers. Not very rational.

However you can see that beliefs which inspire you can play an important part in helping you achieve your goals.

Here are some that I have found useful. I read them every day and I am constantly looking for examples true or fictional stories which show these beliefs to be true.

1. There is always a way
2. I can make this happen
3. I can be whatever I want to be
4. There are opportunities everywhere
5. I love the challenge of business
6. I believe I can make a contribution to the world
7. I can be a millionaire
8. No matter what the problem I can turn it around
9. There is no failure only feedback
10. Money and opportunity are attracted to me

Obviously a track record of success helps anyone to build strong self belief. If you did well at School and were in the first Rugby Team you would have been considered a success – you will believe that you will do well and will act confidently until something major happens in your life to contradict this.

## Be Your Own Coach

There will be time when the world seems against you. If like Samuel you had lost all your money you will suffer from the vagaries of human nature. People will turn on you and will perceive you as a failure. This is part of our culture, whereas in the USA someone who has had a go albeit unsuccessfully is perceived as the type of person who will succeed provided they learn from their mistakes.

Even one empowering belief can be good. However it can help to have someone to believe in you when perhaps you are at your lowest ebb and you start to doubt yourself. Samuel tried hard, picked a poor opportunity and failed in it. As a result business associates family and friends saw him as a person who was no good at business. What was ironic was that some of the doubters had never actually tried any type of venture themselves. In those circumstances unquestioned support and the ability to show the belief "the past does not equal the future" is paramount for success.

We all need mentors.

## Action Plan

There is an entire chapter devoted to being action orientated. Taking small action steps helps to achieve goals, but also helps to build belief as each milestone is reached. You need to tackle a situation and once you establish a small success build on that for the future.

Strong beliefs and values do help to set out where you want to go.

## Positive Memories

Instead of replaying over in your mind situations that went wrong remember when you achieved something you thought impossible. Remember the people who do believe in you. Seek out role models for people who have turned things round and achieved the impossible. What did they say? What did they do? Why did they believe in themselves?

The type of belief I want you to have is a belief in your capabilities, with the ability to visualise yourself achieving the end result. However I do want you to retain some flexibility particularly with regard to strategy. You may have the capabilities and the opportunity to make things happen, but there is always the possibility that your present way of making a project happen is not working no matter what your self belief.

You need to adapt a four stage approach to being a success which underpins a lot of the strategy in this chapter:

1. Know what you want.
2. Take action.
3. Be very aware of the results you are getting.
4. If not change and take a new approach to make things happen.

Belief is challenging when you start off because of the reaction you will get from others who are negative about new innovation type situations. If you have done your homework you need self belief and a belief in your project. I have no doubt that you have excellent potential and are capable of making things happen. However you need to transmit this to other people because they will judge your venture and whether they will back it, with reference to two factors. The competitive advantage of the idea and your capabilities. There are lots of old clichés from the world of positive thinking but it is true that "what you believe you can achieve".

Always believe in yourself but be prepared to learn, adapt, innovate and if necessary change course. Belief also always needs to be backed up by appropriate action. If you have a vision for the long term that is great and will help you with your decisions along the way. It can also be useful to achieve small goals step by step, because the actual achievement will build your belief. This is important for yourself but also for the team you may lead.

Ultimately your beliefs are a self fulfilling prophecy. To quote Henry Ford "if you believe you can you are right. If you believe you can't you are right. It is up to you".

*Task*

What is one new belief you will now use? Do it now!!

## Values

It is important to first of all know what their values are and make sure your projects/businesses/ career are in line with those values. If you are anti nuclear weapons, it does not make a lot of sense to work for the Ministry of Defence. If the company and your values are aligned it increases the chances of successful outcomes.

*Task*

Put the following list of values into order of preference with your highest first: freedom, security, money, health, family, integrity spirituality. Give yourself five minutes.

How did you do? What was first? There is no right or wrong answer. Is health right up on your list? If security is your most important value should you be starting a business in this age of financial uncertainty?

If money is very high up are you working in a career or business that will lead to the financial success you crave? How about if you shifted your values, could that have a positive impact on your performance/contribution? I was reading the "The Apprentice" by Sir Alan Sugar recently, based on the hit TV series, and he made it crystal clear what was his number one value. Family always before business. Yet he seems to have done ok? There are many people who put money first before health or family etc. Health should be high up simply because to remain the enterprising individual you already are, you need a high level of energy and good health. When family, relationships and health are prioritised there is less likely to be a conflict and you can focus on achieving the task in hand.

However do what you feel is right for you. Even if you achieve short term success in a lucrative venture but which is contrary to your values and beliefs there is always going to be a conflict there.

## Motivation

In making anything happen the why is very often more important than the how. When we talk of leadership we will consider the importance of motivating others. However an enterprising person whenever they operate are essentially self starters who will do whatever it takes because of their high level of self motivation.

Your motivation will obviously be helped if you are doing what you love and are good at and believe strongly in what you are doing. However many projects flounder because the key is to remain motivated when there seems to be lack of immediate results or something else intrudes.

## Pain or Pleasure

People are often motivated by either pain or pleasure. They will often take the appropriate action when either they wish to avoid something negative happening or where some appropriate type of reinforce-ment reward could happen. Which works for you? Or is it both? I certainly like to get tangible rewards, financial or otherwise for what I do. However avoidance of major pain seems to be a key driver to get me to take action.

## How Do I Use This?

If you want to make a major change, let us say become more finan-cially successful. You know there are strategies that will help but you never seem to get round to implementing them. For instance three key strategies which could lead to long term financial success would be buying investment property, building up a pension fund, and starting a lucrative business.

My suggestion would be as follows:

1. Imagine yourself in twenty years time; you never got motivated and you still haven't done anything about the key financial strategies. What would your life be like? How would you feel? Imagine your lifestyle. If you visualise this in detail and turn up the pressure, you will begin to feel the pain. No money no pension, no life, no private medical care, no money to support your family no self respect huge regrets no chance to retire or make a contribution.

I'm sorry it is getting quite painful, but if this was the best way to motivate yourself, we could turn the heat up.

If however reward is what motivates you. Imagine the key benefits you will have if you do take action and achieve those financial goals. Imagine no work time to indulge holidays no worries able to help family and friends, good healthcare, freedom to travel, go where you want.

## Short Term

It is also important to do this on a short term basis because the achievement of any long term goal is based on a large number of small steps. It is important that you find your "hot button". What is it that will get you moving?

In selling people will often have great difficulty getting to a sale as often to get one sales interview they may have to ring ten prospects and then have ten interviews to get one sale. Therefore you need to ring 100 suitable prospects to get one sale. How do you motivate yourself for the ninety nine rejections along the way?

Simple, work out what the value of one sale is. Let us say it is £1000. So each of the 100 calls, is worth £10. So each one is another £10 on the way to achieving the goal.

You need to find your why in every project and use that to motivate yourself when times get tough.

Again it could be useful for you to do some simple psychometric tests to help evaluate what motivates you. Talking to family and friends will help.

People who set goals and have a mission will often have a "scrapbook" with pictures of the end goal or some means of bringing this alive. Let us say what they want most of all is a lovely home in the country. Looking at the goals and the visual images once a day will help you realise why you are having all this hassle. Beliefs and values will play apart. Hyrum Smith does a test in his book on values, which asks you for whom would you be prepared to cross a plank 200 yards up to save with the likely risk of losing your own life. ? Your answer may surprise you. Dramatic I know, but effective.

The principles of delayed gratification is a good one, in that you should not always expect rewards to be immediate and in fact you always need to have your strategic vision to hand as the capacity to act now for long term benefits is something you must master. However find simple ways of rewarding yourself for action in the short term. It might be a bath, reading a book etc, you may not consider yourself one of Pavlovs rats but some say there is a bit of a rat in us all!!

## Control Your Emotions

We are all at the mercy of our emotions to a lesser or greater extent. Without wanting to turn you into a machine you need not let emotions control you completely particularly in business.

## Sensitivity

The right type of sensitivity is a good asset in business. Being able to read people and situations and being sensitive to the needs of others can be important for marketing. However being oversensitive to the opinions of others and easily hurt will not help. We are not always able to choose what life throws at us. I do believe we ultimately determine our destiny, but sometimes we are thrown some key situations challenges which do not obviously appear helpful. All you can work on is your reaction to events, and try to turn them round to the advantage of yourself or others. One of the most inspirational one liners I heard recently was from James Boddy a businessman and philanthropist on addressing a group of students "whatever life throws at you get the champagne out" It is not always easy to see the joy in some scenarios which will appear. However you will have a better chance of working with it if you have a positive attitude and realise it is part of your journey/test and you must embrace it and move on with your life. I was particularly impressed by two motivational speakers I heard recently. One had had a leg and a hand blown off in Mozambique whilst working for a mines removal agency. His story of how he searched for his arm/leg and his relief of realising he had something left including his "credentials" was hilarious. If he can react this way why can you not. Mark Pollack who is blind adopts the same attitude. Northern Ireland is similar. Both men continue to physically challenge themselves and inspire other people to face obstacles, and refuse to be beaten.

From somewhere they have got a focus we should all take when dealing with challenges. Ask yourself positive focus questions "what is good about this? What can I learn from this so I can help others? What can I do tot run this to our advantage?

## Controlling State

You all know there are certain times when we feel more powerful and are more likely to achieve results. I believe that physiology plays a part. How are you standing? Are you smiling? What is your body language, change it?

## Relaxation

Your capacity to be enterprising is increased if you can learn to be relaxed. This may seem to be in direct contradiction of many small business courses quite often taken by an employee of a local Enterprise agency who have never ran their own business. They like to advise" For the first five years of business, you must work twenty five hours a day. You can never relax!!" Absolute rubbish. The first skill you should learn is to relax and to make time for it. This helps you deal less emotionally with life's trials.

I don't know if you have ever met someone who practices meditation on a regular basis. Their very presence relaxes you. I read a profile last night of Brian Turtle, Director of BIFHE one of the top three FE colleges in the UK. He explained how he enjoys his work and doesn't worry. If he can relax with the massive financial and business challenges he faces so can you.

The only time you are taught how to relax in this country is when you have a baby. Yet I believe it is the ultimate skill for business.

I think we all realise that momentum is important in business. However relaxed focus can help an individual to concentrate on key issues to by pass stress and make more effective decisions.

*Task*

Find a class or tape teaching relaxation. It could be meditation deep relaxation or self hypnosis. Practice 15 minutes every day. Also spend five minutes every day practising quick relaxation learning to relax muscles and focus on receiving bad news.

This 15-20 minutes every day could change your life. It is also ideal to be in a relaxed state should you want to visualise the achievement of future goals or habit change. Being relaxed helps you visualise with your right brain and stops the incessant analysis and chatter which gets in the way.

### Fears

We are driven by our fears, and although you can't get rid of them completely, you must not let them get in the way of goals. It is right to be afraid of dangerous animals, dangerous road conditions and serious illness. What you have to work on are the irrational fears that hold you back. If we are scared of something or natural reaction is to avoid whatever is causing the fear. People become so skilled at this avoidance that they can end up keeping away from some of the important things in life such as relationships.

Irrational fears can be very extreme after some particularly bad experiences and can almost turn into a "phobia". If you have a fear this extreme you may need to get some professional help.

However you can improve your ability to cope with fears through a number of approaches. Find out what works for you.

### Fear Will Always be There

A lot of approaches get us to accept that the fear is not going away, to accept it but go ahead and do what you have to do. A lot of seminar leaders will get you to do something you never thought possible, like walking on fire. Having found that under the right conditions this was possible to do then you should let go of your fears from now on.

## Have You Any?

Have you any underlying fears that could hold you back? At least admit it to yourself. A few of the key fears may hold you back in enterprise, when you need to take risks. Fear of failure and fear of rejection. Statistics show these are very significant fears which tend to inhibit someone's capability to take action.

You will need to work with this fear if you are going to achieve any significant success. We will discuss this further when we look at personal influence. You will face no's even if you are only asking for people to help you. If you take these no's personally you will quickly become inhibited. Searching for team members, looking for help, selling are all examples where not everything you do will work. As Watson of IBM advised "you need to fail more often".

School does not prepare us to fail, and yet that is how you will learn not only in sales but at every stage of the project. You do not know who is going to help, who is going to hinder and who is going to help you achieve results.

So you have to be relaxed regarding both rejection and failure as in bringing an innovation to life there will be plenty of both. That is where someone who has some type of direct sales experience has an advantage simply through being relaxed about the fact that not every one will support you or everyone will agree.

Geoff Thompson an ex Martial Artist who became an author and a playwright used his own version of "systematic desensitisation" where you grade your fears and gradually work your way through them achieving success at every step.

If you were scared to make a presentation to the Board of Directors of a company for instance, first present to a friend, and then perhaps a small presentation to a group of colleagues, gradually reaching a more challenging audience until you are ready for the Board. Sometimes you may be ready to "jump in at the deep end" and although this type of approach can be very successful you have to be prepared sometimes for it to go wrong and learn from it.

Geoff Thompson's greatest fear was physical confrontation. To overcome it he became a nightclub bouncer and had to deal with it and overcome the fear. However I don't think you need to do anything quite so drastic!!

If you have identified what is the real fear holding you back you are halfway there. Work on your fear, tackle it step by step. Every attempt no matter how small is a major step forward.

In my youth I had a very severe fear of speaking in public after a particularly unsuccessful "mock court debate" in my first year at University. I spent about three years successfully avoiding speaking in front of a group again. Suddenly I was asked to take a one off class at a FE college. I had no choice and was not happy. However the girls, final year A level students were friendly and quite undemanding. I started to believe I could do it and today it holds no fears for me. If an idiot like me can do it so can anyone!!

## Confidence and Self Esteem

You need to learn to like yourself. Again it comes down to programming. If you lack confidence it is not because you were born that way it has a lot to do with environment. Many of us come from well meaning families who do not want us to get above ourselves as children. This can lead to a lack of confidence in our own ability. You need to realise that you have talents and you have every right to be confident in doing something you have experience or ability at. Affirmations can prove useful "I like myself" is a very simple one but effective. "I can and I will" are examples of affirmations that should be repeated on an ongoing basis.

A useful ploy can be when carrying out a task that you do not feel confident about is to act as if you are, you will act differently and get a reaction from your audience. The ironic thing is by moving differently and acting out this role and achieving at least some success you will start to feel more confident yourself.

It is nice to have some cheerleaders in your life. I don't mean in the literal sense!! I am thinking of people who will encourage you. You need to be careful as to who you share your hopes and dreams with. It could be a member of your family, a friend or a mentor at work.

Visualisation can also be a useful strategy. In your daily relaxation session imagine yourself as more confident, acting confidently being the person you want to be. If you could do this for five minutes every day your confidence levels will soar.

You will also have to monitor your self talk. If you have this little voice inside your head which tells you every time you do something wrong "you are useless", you need to change this.

Again change your focus "how can I do better next time?"

Learn to respect yourself, treat yourself just as you would a friend you were trying to encourage and help develop so you can see not only do you have to master communication with the outside world, you have to work on it yourself.

Be careful of the words you use. Let us say you have forgotten to tax your car yesterday "this is a nightmare" is inappropriate use of language. Work on what memories you want to enhance and what you want to forget. If you want to remember a time think of one when you were a big success.

Feel yourself there, create the sounds and the feeling to leave a positive association. If you have had an experience which haunts you and effects your confidence, see it as a distant picture with yourself in it, keep the image dull and lifeless – and free of any emotion. This is to stop the habit we all tend to have of reliving bad memories.

A final strategy can be to remember a time when you acted confidently and were in a good state. Find something visual or a piece of music which you associate with that occasion. Anytime you want to recapture that feeling think of something visual, a sound or feeling which will bring that back.

## Task

Think of a time when you were very confident and were at your best. Turn the sound up, remember what you saw and what you felt. At the peak of the memory touch your thumb and forefinger together. Do the same thing five times. What do you notice?

Work on yourself and be careful on the messages you give yourself. You may have spent years being "modest", thinking this was the way to behave. However confidence is an essential part of your enterprise package. People will respond well to confidence but not arrogance – you can still treat people with consideration and yet be quietly confident.

You need to gradually do more things and be relaxed about the outcome. If you are prepared to take action, relax and learn from your experiences you have every right to be confident. Confidence should be based on the ability to have a go, rather than on someone who never makes mistakes. The attitude you want is "Whatever happens I can turn this around" "I can make this happen". Other people are attracted to confidence and are more likely to support you. Be the best and the most confident you can be. Remember you are only using a small part of your talents/capabilities/brain. Are you interested? Are you prepared to learn? If the answer to these two questions is yes, then be confident.

## Time Management

You will have to challenge any of your habits that reduce your personal effectiveness. Your ability to make use of your time is crucial. A friend sent me a visual representation of the fact that you only have 86400 seconds in a day and that it is the one resource which is going down every day. In that time you want to be successful in your career/business and lead a happy and fulfilling life. There really only seems to be enough time to focus on one or the other.

However you have to work with this valuable resource and get yourself the best deal.

Paretos law applies clearly here. 20% of your time will produce 80% of the results so what are the key priority tasks that you need to focus on.

Sometimes these can be the most difficult tasks, but if you could personally deal with these you might be able to delegate the other 80%. You need to balance your time between things that are urgent now and things that are important. This is difficult, and something that those of you who have your own business will struggle with. There are always so many loose ends to tie up and decisions needed to keep the momentum of a project going. However the strategic use of part of your time can mean less time needed to firefight in the long run.

The power of now is a good philosophy to have in the use of time. If you are at work focus on that the whole time. Do not take long lunch breaks or socialise too much. At the same time when you have blocked out family or recreational time do not let other things intrude. That is what high performers in business do if they are also people who enjoy a happy family and personal life. I know we do advocate working on things you love, but some people use this as an excuse to make work everything, to always be at the office and never really leave it mentally when they come home. If Richard Branson and Alan Sugar always take weekends off surely you can do the same.

**Ability to Say No**

Linked to your ability to assert yourself, you should learn to say no to activities, you are not good at or which intrude on your time.

**Managing Several Tasks**

If you are involved in several projects as I am it can be difficult to know where to start and where to finish. The key again is to set time aside for each task and focus on it. There always has to be a degree of flexibility as unexpected things come up.

**Time Management System**

You need some type of time management system, manual or computerised. Plan your time ahead with a degree of flexibility. Again you want to use the power of leverage to achieve results through the use of other peoples' time. If all you do is sell your time there is a limit to what you can achieve financially or otherwise.

*Chunking*

In project planning it is a good idea to set a timetable and chunk down things into individual bits. As one commentator said "how do you eat an elephant?" a bit at a time.

At the start of each day you need to ask yourself "what can, I do today to move my life forward" and at the end of each day you want to ask yourself the question "what did I do today? What contributions did I make?

There can be a tendency to rule out community activities thinking there will be plenty of time later for that when you retire. However you do not know how long you have got. So making a contribution without looking for a return can add immeasurably to your life and give you a perspective on things. I was particularly taken by a social enterprise set up in my own area by a church. They have created a modern trendy café with all profits going to third world enterprises and with an ongoing commitment to running community activities at the café as part of the ethos of the enterprise.

**Relaxed Focus Momentum**

Time taken to relax (remember your fifteen minutes every day) is also time well spent. It will improve your creativity and reduce stress levels. Spending time relaxing and taking exercise are very strategic as bad health can undermine all your activity. No matter how efficient you are there is always room for improvement.

## Momentum

As well as your "timeouts" it is important to live every day as if it should not be wasted. An example I heard was how you would use your time if you were told if you were able to clear your work up over the next few days a helicopter would be coming to take you to Acapulco. Would it concentrate your mind? Sadly many of us only tend to work that way near urgent deadlines. We enjoy the adrenalin rush but the sad thing is normally we are wasting a lot of our time.

### Task

Keep a time log for a week, work out where you spend a lot of your time. Is there anything you would like to change? How much time are you spending on strategic long term things?

Time moves on and you can't go back. Make sure you are spending time on what is important for you. I am the one showing you how to be more enterprising. However it should not be at the expense of the rest of your life.

My belief is that the enterprising person values time and makes the best use of it. You have heard the old adage, give a busy man something to do. Some people get through so much in a day in all aspects of their life. Others never seem to have time for anything.

Time is a resource, possibly the ultimate resource you need to value it in all aspects of your life. Don't follow the example of the author who once paid £150 for a time management course but did not have the time to go on it.

There are no magical systems but have one which works for you – surely one of your aims is to make the best use of your time now so that your business and family will both benefit in the long run. I see examples of people who have got the time equation wrong – successful business men in their 70s who are still working 60 hrs a week or bored pensioners who retire early and without the value of work fill their time by watching soaps on the TV.

There is a tendency to live each day the same and think that you have as much time as possible. Having lost a very close relative recently who I rarely got to see because I was too busy, I wish I could go back and change how I spent that time. However as Omar Kyhaim the ancient poet said "the moving finger having writ moves on". "Nor all their piety nor all thy wit shall change a single word of it" food for thought.

*Task*

What 2 things could you change now to make the best use of your time.

## Health

I am the last person to lecture anyone on health. I do realise that most high performers have a lot of energy to achieve what they do. You need to watch diet and exercise. 15 minutes of exercise four times a week, a diet relatively low in carbohydrate and fat and your ongoing relaxation will all help with stress. There is an optimal level where you can enjoy stress but beyond a certain point it can cause difficulties and high blood pressure is something to monitor. Regular health checks are also important. There is a tendency only to get there when suddenly we don't feel well but again proactivity is what matters.

For those of you who are at the early stage of your career it is hard for you to take health habits too seriously. However although the wrong habits do not affect you now, those habits will be difficult to shift later on.

## Strategic

Try and look long term and short term on anything you are working on. A friend of mine was saying the other day that she had noticed in middle age that the people who had knuckled down to get qualifications or experience early on were reaping the dividends in career terms now.

Unfortunately even now public sector organisations are always having performance measured by short term budgetary performance. Is there anything you can spend time on now which will help you in the long run.?

## Personal Development

The focus of this chapter is on helping you to develop your potential and in challenging the enemy within. Unfortunately we all have aspects of our personality that we would like to change. There are a lot of people who think personal development is "bunkum" and want to ignore it. There are others who attend every personal development course available and tend to build their favourite authors/speakers into guru status. However they do not change and keep spending more and more on the gurus course convinced they will eventually get the secret.

There are many factors that have made us the person we are. To have any hope of change firstly you must want to and have a strong desire. Secondly you have to accept that you will not change overnight but instead that you are on a journey and it will at times seem very like one step forward and one step back.

This is particularly frustrating if you acquire great knowledge of how to change, want to share it with others but never get round to doing it yourself. The most effective teaching is not delivering a lecture but being a model for someone else because you have integrity and do what you say you are going to do.

The key to personal mastery is the ability to be self aware and to seek feedback from people you trust. The annoying thing (tell me about it) is it is much easier to help other people change than to do it yourself. Accept you are human and although you will not always "walk your talk" you will do your best.

There is no system that works for everyone. You will come across people who will advocate positive thinking, therapy or the works of one particular guru. However there are no set answers and basically all these models teach the same basic principle. Relax, visualise, build your self esteem. Learn to control your emotions and take action. There is no set length of time it will take. However do prepare a personal development plan.

*Task*

What aspect of your behaviour would you like to change now? Work on it. Some changes will be easier than others but even small changes make a big difference. The premise of this book is that you are only as strong as your weakest area. Work on it, improve it a little and you will leverage the effect on you life as a whole.

Find you way to be the best you can be. It is also important that whatever your career success be yourself. Be authentic. There is nothing harder than being true to yourself to make changes and develop as your life goes on. You will develop and change no matter how you try, just make sure your changes are appropriate.

Be in control of your development and know not only where you want to end up but what type of person you can be. Success can be just as much of a challenge as failure. Are you still your same old self?, As you develop on the E Factor and move forward even though you are now a multimillionaire, a success in conventional terms, don't change. Underneath you are still the same person who respects other people and will never sell out to the establishment. Let us say Develop and remain the same. Quite a challenge!

# — 3 —

# ASSERTION/NEGOTIATION

## ASSERTION

I believe your ability to assert yourself and negotiate to be one of the core competencies of Enterprise.

I do however have a confession to make, as like everyone some of my E Factor scores are better than others.

I have been proactive and been good at goal achievement and have even been accused of being "pushy" in the past. However I am not naturally very good at dealing with aggression I hate confrontation and will not always speak up as I should. I also am not very good at saying no. These are all areas that I have had to work on. The whole point of E Factor is to work on all areas but particularly on a weakness which could block your progress. I found to my cost several times in business that "niceness" can be perceived as weakness.

You have to find your own communication style that works but it is something I practice every day. I keep a journal and record every day my victories and defeats.

Assertion is therefore one of the 20% of activities that will make 80% of difference in my activities. When I am ready I am looking forward to in particular leading assertion classes. In other areas such as finance or creativity I have developed the skills but assertion is an area where I have been like a recovering alcoholic and may be able to contribute more in the future, as I know where people are coming from

Now read on!! (only joking)

### So What Is Assertion?

Assertion is standing up for your rights without hurting anyone else. Aggression is where you are prepared to "walk over the top" of someone else to get what you want. Timidity is where you do not stand up for your rights and let others do whatever they want. People often confuse aggression with assertion.

You will find a lot of aggressive people in business and therefore the myth is perpetuated that this is the way you must be to succeed in business and people even if they don't feel natural try to follow this model.

However if you do not consider the rights of other people and are overly aggressive do not expect to deal with that person or business a second time. You may be met with opposition straight away or even if you have won a victory there is a cost. The ideal model has got to be "win win" where you try if possible to create a deal where both sides get something.

However lets be honest it is better to be aggressive than to be too nice and to let other people always have the upper hand. It is an unfortunate aspect of human nature that people will take advantage of this.

What you will find is that your style of communication will vary with the different groups you communicate with. It is partly the situations, we find ourselves in which can lead to different responses

For instance an aggressive manager at work may be too unassertive at home with his children as he want to overindulge their every whim through guilt at working too much. The assertive schoolteacher may have no problem at school but be unable to assert themselves with their mother in law.

### Why Are We Assertive/Aggressive?

Again our programming and out environment has played a part. Sometimes as parents we want our children to be obedient and do what they are told. School rules can also follow the same format. This can lead the model child to become a "yes man" as an adult and to have difficulty with authority figures. Again it is a learned skill. Everyone needs to learn to be independent and to be proactive in seeking their own rights.

At the same time aggression is increasing in our culture. The problem with being too nice is that avoiding conflict and keeping the peace can lead to resentment and potential aggression in the long run.

You need to learn to say no. For some it is all they can say but politeness can go hand and in hand with always saying yes. However you must learn to stand up for yourself and get what you want. That is what negotiation is about. Life consists of a series of deals with family, friends and business contacts. If you constantly take less than 5% of every deal you do not get what you deserve and are driven by the fear of consequences. The danger is this can become a serious liability. What I hope my suggestions will do is to give you a framework to practice the middle ground behaviour.

When you are a child your parents or even big brothers/sisters are there to stick up for you. When you are an adult you have to adopt this role ourselves. What you earn, how your life and business runs depends to a certain extent on your assertion skills. It is also a part of a good direct method of communicating with others. Other people will tread on your toes and try to take advantage sometimes without fully intending to. If you do not let them know directly you are creating difficulties. It is bad enough not getting a fair deal. However sometimes non assertive people will still want their way and will try to do it indirectly. They will manipulate and cajole and can be seen as devious because they are not upfront with their feelings/thoughts. Obviously although honest communication is desirable some form of subtlety is required. Still people feel comfortable dealing with someone with whom they know where they are with. If they make a deal whatever the terms they like to think that both parties will stick to it.

*Assertion Task*

Here is an assertion checklist. Please tick the areas you have problems with. Those of you who are much too aggressive are likely to have the most difficulty in recognising you have a problem because after all you are never wrong!!

Checklist             ✓ to agree

1. I can never say no
2. I hate confrontation
3. I am too aggressive
4. I want to be liked
5. I hate rejection
6. I don't like speaking up
7. I will put up with a lot
8. I put myself down
9. I find it difficult to cope with other people's aggression
10. I don't like to make a fuss

If you have ticked (1-3) of the areas you have work to do. If all of them you will need to develop an assertion plan. If none of them, congratulations. If you are not sure get feedback from others you can trust. People with assertion problems either believe they can't stand up for themselves at all or are blissfully unaware they have a problem, and take pride in their aggression.

The best communicator is the most flexible. If you want to build rapport with the other side in a negotiation sometimes a more laid back but firm style will work, sometimes you need to show the same level of assertion but adopt a strong approach.

## Everyday Life

The beauty of assertion is that you can practice it in every day life. You maybe want to build up to asking your boss for a raise or to dealing with a difficult workmate, so you can start off with much simpler tasks, sending food back in a restaurant or saying no to someone who is trying to sell something in the street. I think I have got too good at this skill, no-one selling something in the street ever seems to approach me.

Small victories and defeats matter. Record them and learn what you did wrong.

## Rehearsal

If you have for instance an interview presentation or a difficult meeting coming up; it can be useful to roleplay with a friend. Do this a couple of times and you will be better in the real situation.

## Body Language/Tonality

In putting your point across it is important that you are congruent. As you know words only convey 5% of the meaning. The other 95% will be conveyed by tonality and body language. You may manage to say "no" but the full communication must show that you mean business; that you mean what you say. Again you will have practice getting this "congruency" across. If you will carry out roleplays and rehearsals., this will help There is nothing however to beat a real life situation. It may only be telling your friends that you can't put them up on Saturday night, not when you need to confront your business partner about an irregularity in the accounts but it is a start.

What is important is doing the work that will eventually lead to you being yourself and say what you feel no matter who you are dealing with.

Some of you may have great assertion skills in many areas but fail miserably in one or two other areas, which create real problems for you.

## Is This a Women's Issue?

Assertiveness is quite often taught in women's personal development courses but it is a problem which exists both in men and women.

### Task 2

Identify the situations/ types of people where you have difficulty being assertive.

Which are the most critical? Pick one which you can work towards.

It is important that you do understand how you came to be the way you are and where it is a liability. I also want you to feel you can make a choice and take action.

## Are You Wrong Being Too Nice?

To be agreeable, helpful or considerate will go a long way. For those of you who are too aggressive and wonder why you get people's backs up, you can learn a lot Some. people will try to solve problems and be agreeable. However it is not always appropriate to be nice and in particular when you would prefer to act differently and also know that you need to act differently but can't.

What type of situations can this include? For instance if someone is trying to "walk over the top of you" or insult you or your work there is a need to be direct. If you feel powerless in this type of situation, that is definitely a liability. You need to realise that if you are always too nice people get fed up with your indecision. They also can consider you "too nice to be wholesome". Someone recently who would ask my opinion on their work performance got a little fed up when I gave my usual "nice" response, would say "you never give an honest opinion".

## Should Everyone Like You?

It is unlikely that everyone will like you. Some people will dislike you without even knowing you and it can be a shock for us "people players". I remember as a graduate entrant in National Westminster Bank, being put into a local branch to "learn the trade" being hated for being a graduate on an accelerated scheme and for being Irish. The answer was to be relaxed, focus on work performance accepting that people will take time to get to know the real you.

*Task 3*

Your boss has given you a report to finish. You are really struggling and are not going to meet the deadline. Should you talk to him?

## Answer

The passive person is likely to think of the worst consequences and be scared of what is going to happen. You are coming up with your own rules, shoulds and musts. You should talk to him having decided what outcome you want for the meeting.

## Telling the People

There are a few people who are genuinely nice all the time but many people feel anger, want to confront the person who has caused it, but instead they talk to third parties. Why? Sometimes they can be scared of triggering off somebody's anger. It can be shocking to realise that other people do not have the same map of the world as you; they don't worry about offending people before they say what they think. People do not have to conform to your expectations and way of behaviour. The only person's behaviour you can change is your own. It is important that you act as you feel, and are not on the outside this person with no opinions and who is always nice but inwardly seething about everything. It is bad for your health, and self esteem.

## Why Am I That Way?

You were certainly not born too passive. Babies are naturally asser-tive to get their needs met. It is likely that it came from your environment particularly from your family. My mother god rest her soul was a very good and kind individual. Like all parents there is no training that goes with the job – we do the best we can. My father was very bad tempered and although he was different with at least one of my sisters, he did not accept answering back. The first time I answered my father back I was twenty. As a result when people in authority or aggressive people try to bulldoze me into doing things I shouldn't do, my natural inclination is to say yes to please them. This is an example of twenty years programming. New behaviour has to be practiced to get a different result.

## Task 4

Is there anything in your childhood, family/school situation that could explain some of your assertion hang ups?

## Fear of Consequences

Your imagination can run riot. If I tell this customer I can't do this work they will get angry they will go elsewhere. It is true that some-times people will react as you anticipate. The problem for you is you imagine it is going to happen everytime.

## The Fight or Fight Syndrome

These are two primitive responses which are in us all. Fight is the primitive response where you get ready to defend yourself. Flight can mean where you continually walk away from a situation where there could be a confrontation. Again sometimes it can be good to get a clear head, and sometimes you are making things worse.

It is difficult to control the feelings. What you have to deal with is what happens next. What you need to do is change your focus response from for instance, a sick feeling in your stomach when you want to stand up for yourself.

You should ask yourself a focusing question "how can I take action here?"

## Anger

We all feel anger some time or other. Do you explode or implode? Neither is particularly good and yet anger is a natural emotion.

The problem is if you are nice when you should not be, you are going to be put upon. If this goes on too long you will go straight to "nasty temper".

The problem with this is that you could create a mess.

The challenge is if your behaviour is like going up and down the gears of a car. At the minute you are either in first or fifth and never in between. You should be able to change your speed to suit the road conditions. You need to change your behaviour to suit the type of person and situation you face. If your child is in physical danger that is not the time for passive Mr Nice. People are not deliberately trying to hurt you when they are needing something done, but in getting something done people will look for the most accommodating. Start to be aware if you are giving off any signals which say "choose me". Look to make small changes that give you a better chance of operating effectiveness.

## It's All a Game

To change your behaviour to improve any of the E Factors you need to practice. The first time you use any of the strategies it will probably not work. However enjoy it, it is a game you are playing.

What is difficult about behaviour like assertion is that once you start to use some of the strategies you will come up against resistance at all sides. Your friends and family who are used to taking advantage of you won't like the new you.

## Watch Your Language

The words you use to communicate are unfortunate. Don't over apologise, It's the little phrases like "I'm so sorry to ask you this" that can dilute the message you are trying to give. Start to observe both the internal chat in your head and how you speak to others.

## Stop!

Every time you tell yourself off say to yourself stop! Ask yourself the question, "how can I prove myself here?"

## Task

Next time you catch yourself apologising for nothing or using passive language say "stop!"

## Strategies

Certain things are important when you are being assertive, maintaining eye contact, not smiling, not getting drawn into a conversation and keeping the conversation as short as possible.

## The Status Quo

In work or within a business there always seems to be a pecking order. People tend to treat people according to their status without a formal or informal network. The ironic thing is that every day you will alter your behaviour depending on who you are with. Quite often you will vary your body language, tonality and words.

Where appropriate you have to act to raise your status.

Someone with high status

1. takes their time
2. uses silence
3. listen without comment
4. maintain eye contact

You can also lower your status for effect.

Let us say you have a friend who earns less than you and has got used to you helping them out. If they are constantly trying to manipulate you lower your status, play them at their own game, use sympathy, show you support their position and wish you could help if only you can afford it.

## Play the Numbers

Always remember you have a choice to play, 10 (high status) or 1 (low status).

It is important to sometimes change the status level to be assertive in the appropriate way. Hopefully with this no doubt you will get it wrong a few times but you will learn.

## Don't Rise to the Bait

People have learned what buttons to press to manipulate you. Have fun learning how to avoid them.

## Practice

Deliberately have nice days when you are sweetness and light and not so nice days where you are more direct and forthright.

Look for any opportunity no matter how small to practice the skills.

There is no need to change your personality or what you are. Remain "nice" but someone nice with an edge who can adapt to circumstances and different people and communicate properly.

I cannot emphasise enough how the use of some of these materials could change your enterprise performance by itself. People trying to encourage enterprise spend a lot of money giving people help on business fundamentals and on completing their business plan. However they need to realise that this help will go to waste if the budding entrepreneur is unable to be assertive. Let me show you the areas where a lack of assertion can count against the enterprising person.

1. Being given a poor deal by their bank manager
2. Being bullied by suppliers and customers
3. Customers taking too long to pay
4. Paying too much for everything
5. Conflict with partners
6. Breaching ethical rules to please customers
7. Being too aggressive to everyone
8. Being bullied by government agencies

The list goes on in business you will come across aggressive business people who will try to win at any cost. Government agencies who will bully you difficult customers, suppliers and staff who will try to impose their rules on you; you will need to stand up for your business or you will not survive. You will need to be assertive with professional advisers who do what you say and who don't try to bully you in their professional role.

## NEGOTIATION

### Introduction

Negotiation is a process and has some similarity to sales which is covered in personal influence. Sales is really one type of negotiation, as you make deals in every aspect of your business. In doing the deal you need to assert your rights otherwise you will get a poor deal, lose money or lose ground.

I have found it to be a core business and life skill, and yet again something which is not taught in the academic curriculum.

### "Everything is Negotiable"

Gavin Kennedy an Edinburgh Professor wrote a book with this title. It is a good mindset. We can all believe in fixed procedures, set rules or set prices, but they should be challenged.

### There is No Set Price

There are no set prices. Some of us love to haggle naturally for others it is an embarrassment. However if you don't ask you don't get. It all depends on the deal. Suppliers may be prepared to reduce the price of product if there are other certainties/favourable points built into the deal.

### "The Art of the Deal"

This is the name of a book written by Donald Trump who spends most of his life putting together property deals. It is more of an art than a science. You need to learn to find your own style that works for you. The traditional negotiation model is of "playing aggressive hardball". However that may not be suitable in the circumstances or not be your style.

### Do Your Homework

As with sales you need to prepare before the deal. You need your technical data and you need to know the personalities and what are their key objectives.

You will also learn a lot face to face during the negotiation. You will sense how much the other party wants to deal and on that basis can decide your own strategy.

## The Deals You Make Are the Life You Make

Your career/enterprise is very dependent on your deal making capabilities. Your relationships are also a deal, and you have got to strike a fair compromise.

It is very easy to get the deal wrong. If a key condition or pricing structure is left out, the whole deal can fail.

## Decide What You Want

You need to know what outcomes you must have, and what are desirable as you may be required to trade something.

## Rapport and Understanding

It is important to build some sort of rapport. You need to spend time getting to know each other and your positions. You are unlikely to agree with the other sides perspective, but it is useful to seek to understand it and to try if possible to be "win win". If you try to get everything you create bad relationship, no further deals and a reputation as someone who has to take everything in the deal. There is strategic value in giving the other side something.

## Decide Where to Start and Where to End

If you start off by stating exactly what you want you will end up getting less. People will usually pitch lower until they see the position.

## Be Prepared to Walk Away

It will always be to your advantage if you are genuinely prepared to walk away if the deal is not right. The other party will remember this and it will strengthen your position.

## Get the Deal in Writing

A lot of older business people like to think when they have shook on a deal that the transaction is sacrosanct – you always need a written signed contract to spell things out, in the event of any future dispute.

## Don't Take Things Personally

Things may be said during a negotiation that can normally lead to offence being taken. A negotiation is no time to be too sensitive and your ability to remain relaxed but focused on the outcome is critical.

## Creativity

A negotiation is not a time to stick to one position only. You may have fall back positions but your challenge is to sometimes find a lateral position particularly where there is deadlock.

## Who Has the Leverage?

Who has the strongest position? If it is you make sure you use whatever leverage you can use. If the other party has it, giving up is not the best option. The best negotiators even if in a weak position can sometimes make the positions seem more balanced simply because of their position. I remember a small business client who had a £30,000 unsecured overdraft and was therefore in serious trouble berating his Bank Manager for not looking after her properly. If you refer to the orientation material you need to adopt an appropriate status behaviour.

### Review their Perceptual Position

People do see things differently. Your ability to see things from other people's perceptual position is important.

*Task*

Take time out. Think of a situation where you are at loggerheads with someone else. Imagine you are the other person, what are you thinking?, what do you want out of the negotiation?. Change and become a third person not involved in the deal. How do you see it?, sitting on the outside, what do both parties want? How can you help?

### Do Not Accept their First Offer

This is the worst thing to do. Not only is it likely to be their "worst offer" but the other party will expect you to haggle. In fact by accepting someone's first offer you will make them worried that they have got it wrong.

I can't emphasise that once the first offer is made, that is when the dealing is done. For instance at one stage of my career I got a job I really wanted and needed. I wasn't particularly happy with the pay-ment but immediately accepted thinking I would easily up my package once I was in the organisation. I found to my dismay that this was not how it worked. The time to sort out the deal was now over after they showed they wanted me to join. It was accepted prac-tice.

### Look for Tradeoffs

If you have a grievance focus on getting something more from the deal.

## What If?

This is your key question to ask when making the deal. It is too late to ask afterwards. You have to get answers to all sorts of contingencies and change the deal to reflect it.

## Learn to Enjoy It

Research I have carried out on top negotiators show that they love to deal. It may not come naturally to you and you may find it embarrassing initially; rest assured if you don't or won't negotiate you will get much less out of life financially or otherwise.

You need to learn to enjoy it. Negotiation is a game and you can simply get better by playing the game. Let us say you are getting a new cleaner for your house. Practice deal making, make sure you get a fair deal. Work up to where you could negotiate with your bank manager or boss at work.

## Reputation

Work on your business reputation. Deals will be much easier for you if you have the right reputation "hard but fair" is the type of reputation you want. The reputation of very easy to deal with" can leave you with a reputation as a pushover. If you constantly make deals and then don't stick to them this will run your credibility in negotiations.

How do you get this reputation? Two ways:

1.  How you have handled previous negotiations
2.  PR

We talk in the book about your personal marketing. It is important to think through how you present yourself as that is how you are perceived.

## The Details

All details matter. This can include everything from what you wear to where the venue is. This should all be included in your planning. However details will emerge which may change the structure of the deal. Be prepared to use that to your advantage.

*Task 2*

Go out and search for a consumer item such as a new TV. Use this situation as a chance to negotiate a deal. Unless you want to buy it at the end of the negotiation say you will go back and think about it. Practice your skills. It is preferable if it is something you want, but there is no practice like the real thing.

What did you learn?

## Review

What we need you to overcome is the embarrassment of asking for a reduction or a change in a deal, particularly when the other side like to make you believe that the terms are fixed. When you make someone a really low offer for something with a high mark up they will be shocked and possibly initially angry.

You hear people using the phrase "I won't insult you with a silly offer". Good business people are not afraid to make low offers, particularly if they are used to buying and selling. They believe that you can make an offer as low as you like, and sell as high as they like.

One author recommends you go into an electrical goods shop where you see a TV priced say for £500. Walk up to the salesman and offer him £30 just to get used to the reaction.

I am not recommending that you always aim to take advantage of people but you must get used to the fact that in many cases people will value their products, services and assets much greater than you do. Unless your aim is to get people to like you, constantly pay over the odds and lose money, you are going to have to negotiate.

There may be occasions when you bring someone in to negotiate on your behalf, but it is not practical to do so all the time. As life is a series of deals the ability to negotiate is high.

## Posture

It is important that you get your posture right. Opponents are looking for signs of weakness, over eagerness to agree. If you appear too arrogant or aggressive there is a danger of alienating the negotiator or their advisor.

The element of surprise can be useful, particularly where the other negotiators are overplaying the status card. Inland Revenue investigators expect Businessmen to be on the defensive. Usually there is something to hide and the cards all seem to be stacked in the favour of the investigators who have strong powers and adopt a very threatening posture. Accountants will usually be compliant because a lot of their work will depend on their relationship with the Inland Revenue so they will tend not to be too assertive.

This is not really fair representation for the businessman. One businessman had quite an innovative approach to these negotiations. He brought in a top QC to the meeting, who was not even a tax barrister.

What he did was turn the table, i.e. started asking the investigators questions and forced them to adopt a different approach. I am not criticising the Inland Revenue but showing it as an example of how parties will often act a certain way if they have status control. The ironic thing is that good negotiators are like poker players and you never guess that on paper they are at a severe disadvantage on negotiations.

## Attention to Detail

Like much of business the deal is in the details. That is why using the "what if" questions can be useful. If there is not enough clarification a minor point can be crucial later on. In an ideal world the deal should be run through a piece of software that could pick up the potential for miscommunication and conflict.

## Opening Offers

Your opening offer is crucial. If you are too near to what you really want you will end up nowhere near it as in many cases the offer will be seen as an opening gambit and the other party will hope to get a much better deal. It may be better to make a tough opening offer provided it is still credible. You need to convince the seller that you still want to genuinely buy their product. It is also a good idea if you can convince the seller you do not have the funds to meet their opening offer.

You do need to be tough and refuse to be intimidated. You should never be giving one way concessions without getting something back. What you are trying to get across is a psychological message. If you want something it is going to cost you.

## Posture Part 2

I do sympathise well maybe only for a moment with possible bargaining positions you find yourself in. If you are applying for your first job after University, you desperately want to get into publishing and this is the only offer you have received; or you have started a small business organising events. You have got no business in your first three months and now a local council has asked you to organise their Halloween firework display. Your natural response is "where do I bite their hand off"?

However the negotiating part has two agendas. They don't want to overpay. However they expect any candidate worth their salt to negotiate. If they don't they worry whether they will be able to carry out the project the way it should be. Get the deal on the wrong terms you will find it hard to increase your salary or your price for future council projects. Yes there may be some deals or opportunities lost but much greater potential that when you get deals, you will get the right one. You cannot do every deal. I am reminded of an old John West Salmon advertisement "It is the fish that John West reject that makes John West the best". Some of the best deal making you do will be the deals you walk away from.

For instance everyone is into buy to let property and as a result there have been significant house rises and a great difficulty at the moment within the UK in getting rental returns to pay mortgage interest and expenses. So if you are a good business person you have got to search through a lot of bad deals to find the ones that are self funding. If you can make property deals that self fund you can do more. If you are having to pay part of the mortgage yourself and want to do more similar deals hoping for long term appreciation, your cash flow is potentially catastrophic. Your deal making skills come into play and you should never give anyone more power or leverage. Something it is natural to always assume the other party has something up their sleeve or hold all the cards. Sometimes it may be true, but often most of it is in the mind.

### Remember Price is Not the Only Issue

As well as price in any deal you will have a number of related items products/services peripherals; the terms related to which could also be negotiated in the deal.

### Keep Your Options Open

It is always good to have other options, other than feeling under threat. If you are trying to up the price your major customer pays, you need to have sought out alternatives and if necessary be prepared to walk away if they refuse to budge. I always find it amazing how attractive an employee can become to an employer, when other people are offering them better packages to go and work for them. Again perception is important, and like much of your achievement a lot will depend not on the actual reality but how you value yourself because that is likely to be how others will value you as well. In an ideal world people will give you as much as you deserve, but that is not how it works in practice. If you want anything you have to ask for it.

I think we should end this section by looking at a short case study relating to negotiation and assertion to illustrate it is one of the core competencies you must develop. You may not be a capitalist but if you want to make things happen you will need to work with other people gather resources and implement. All stages require negotiation skills. Are you working on yours?

### Case Study

Jean has been taken on as a graduate trainee by a local charity for the disabled. They want her to run a new project to raise £250,000 a year for the charity and to build up the volunteer base and corporate sponsorship for the charity. What situations and issues will Jean face where she may need her negotiation skills? (please spend 10 minutes on your answer before turning over).

### Some Thoughts

Jean has got to be enterprising to set up a new innovative project and make it happen. Will she have to negotiate anything? Almost everything:

1. First of all she needs to agree the terms of your contract. Is it fixed term or permanent? What is her salary and benefit package?
2. Jean needs to agree with her boss exactly what outcomes have to be achieved and within what timescale
3. Jean needs to establish what resources are available. Does she have a marketing budget? Does she have the help of any paid or volunteer staff?
4. Jean has to negotiate some type of reward systems if she makes the project successful

5. Jean has to do deals with local companies and give them some key benefit they are seeking in return for their financial contribution.

6. Jean will design some type of deal for volunteers and look for negotiable benefits which might attract volunteers.

7. Jean will need to do deals with stakeholders in all stages of the projects

8. Jean should identify alternative sources of funding and negotiate a package which may fund the operation pending corporate or fund raising events

9. Jean will look at what deals could bring in the £250,000 and negotiate terms and conditions

10. Jean will need to negotiate with friends and family to get their support in her new job.

## Conclusion

Hopefully you can see just because an area of work is not obviously a business venture, this does not preclude the need for negotiation. Some people seem to be born dealmakers. When I was nine I used to buy a quarter of sweets, take them to church and in the children's church sell sweets for the children's collection. This happened for three weeks until the helper put a stop to it. I was doing deals but actually as I focused more and more on my schoolwork, I didn't really build my dealing skills. As someone who just wants the job done, it is easy to do poor deals just to move a project on. However like many other people I have had to realise that almost anything in life is dependent upon a deal. If the deal is right everything will flow. Make a bad deal in business or personal life, and despite your best efforts, things will not work.

## Observation

As well as practising some of the ideas contained here, I recommend you start observing people, and only dealing/bartering situation. If you find something useful try to apply it straight away.

Keep a mini record of your new negotiation life. Review every deal you make, no matter how small. What can you learn from this? You can also do deals on behalf of others. The ironic thing is because you are a third party and not emotionally involved you will do better deals for them than you do for yourself.

Never accept anything if people have favours or requests to make of you, what do you need from them?

At time we have been advocating a fairly hardnosed approach. However I am still not a fan of taking 100% and leaving the other party nothing. They are less likely to stick to the deal, and at the very best will tend to badmouth you. Try to be strategic don't shoot yourself in the foot in the long run.

Try to be honourable but that does not mean saying yes to deals that don't suit you or are unfair. Every deal is different, will progress at different rates and will have its own subtle nuances. You need to apply the basic success principle. Know what you want before you start, do the negotiations, decide where to make the pitch and be flexible. Try to change what you can offer if there are particular needs and you are still getting what you want. Flexibility is the key and that includes getting out. Develop negotiation skills and I promise you, you will be welcome in any industry and will fare much better. In an ideal world the meek should prosper in our world business or personal, but always remember "blessed is the dealmaker"!!

# — 4 —

# PERSONAL MARKETING

## PERSONAL MARKETING

Marketing is not just a function needed by large or small corporates. It is an attitude of mind in which your company or organisation sets out to meet the needs of a defined market and organises all the activities of the company to meet them. You need to think of yourself as a company, a personal services company.

Whether you are setting up a business or working for a company, you are a one man/woman personal services company and you need to use the concepts of marketing to get yourself the best deal in the marketplace.

## What are these Marketing Concepts?

You need to do ongoing market research, develop your own marketing mix to achieve your goals. There is an interesting book in America where a marketing consultant applies marketing concepts to the mission of finding a suitable husband or wife. This is not my arena but its success as a bestseller illustrates the recognition that marketing techniques can be used in your career or business. It may also illustrate how desperate some people are to find a partner!!

## You are the Brand?

Everyone knows about the Beckham brand. The couple are recognised as a worldwide brand because they have been marketed as such. Everything you do, wear or say adds to the perception other people have of you. You need to clear what image/impression you want to give and make sure you don't get involved in activities which conflict with the market you are aiming to reach.

I came across a young lawyer who was aiming to build a practice with large established customers in a local town. The image he needed to project was that of someone business like, a safe pair of hands respected in the local community.

To his cost he got involved in a "get rich quick" scheme which involved getting other people signing up and buying stock. Clients who came into his office to get advice about their legal structure found themselves being harangued to join the scheme. The young lawyer as is often the case didn't make any money out of the get rich quick scheme. More importantly the young lawyer was not seen as the safe pair of hands any more. It was a big blow to his long term prospects of gaining any kind of local market share.

### Task

What type of brand image do you want to project: who is your customer?

Let us say for instance you want to appeal to one of the major consultancies such as Accenture. You need to find out early on what type of person they are looking for and what evidence would be useful. If you found for instance they wanted someone enterprising who could take responsibility for projects, you would look at your track record and you could consider becoming an intern for the student enterprise centre and look for some student activities such as the Faculty formal where you could take responsibility for making it happen.

The difficulty with this strategy is that you must still be sure that you are not trying to change your personality and activities just to get a job for a company which you are not suited for. It can seem to go against the advice "be yourself". The point is, it is important to recognise what you are interested in and good at, but use marketing strategies to achieve what you want. You may not be the greatest talent the publishing industry has been looking for, but if they don't become aware of you and you don't get yourself into a position to show that you can make a contribution, you have no chance. Many of you will be brought up to keep out of the limelight and not to put yourself forward. However it is a very competitive world and you need to get a competitive advantage.

## Market Research

If you are building a business, not only do you need to assess market need at the start of the business but it is an ongoing process. Markets will change and you need to change the focus of your products or services to meet changing requirements. The same applies to corporate or community careers. What are the key qualities needed? What does the market need?

Not only do you need to show market awareness of whatever industry you are in, you need to know what the employment and business market is looking for. For instance many businesses and companies want their new graduates to be enterprising and innovative. How can you demonstrate these qualities and your capacity to act that way in the job situation? Are there courses being run in innovation? what type of work experience would could you get in the holidays?

Market research information can be got both formally and informally. Read market reports on the trends in your industry, find out what statistical data says about the size of the market for your product. Informal information can also be useful. Knowing what is a key driver for a chief buyer in a major company or what are the major preferences of the recruitment team. I found informal information to be very useful prior to an interview for my first job in accountancy with a major industrial company. This was my one opportunity to get into an excellent training scheme. Informal information gathering allowed me to find out that the main recruiter was focused on all student trainee accountants being committed to qualifying. It was very useful to know this – I was genuinely committed to doing this but knowing his key preference helped in marketing my services.

Whatever your business ambitions you need to have access to information. Building networks will help as well as awareness of published market research available. You must not ignore what the market tells you. That is the main principal of marketing which separates it from selling.

What are your customers or potential customers saying? What needs/benefits do they have? Will they still be looking for the same thing in the long term? Do their needs/benefits match with the product service you offer.? If not what value can you add to your offering to make it more likely that you can do business? If you can't you may need to look at the market and look for a different niche to pursue.

The market research information is only of any use if you will base your activities on it. Never assume because you are in business or have experience of an industry that you know all the answers, you need to ask the market, respect it and adjust your marketing plan accordingly. You also must keep abreast of developments and respond appropriately. As a small business if you do not respond to changes your business is in trouble. Your marketing should be more about making a sale or getting that job. It should be strategic. If you are the product where are you on the product cycle? Where will the market be in five years time? Will you be strategically positioning yourself to take advantage of opportunities that will become available?

*Task*

What market information do you need? How can you get it without any major financial or time implication?

## SWOT Analysis

This is a standard analysis companies will do as regards their product offerings, strengths, weaknesses, opportunities and threats. Still keeping on the theme that you are the product in personal marketing it is important to analyse where you are as regards the market having already done your market research.

What are your strengths with regard to the opportunity offered? What are your weaknesses? What are the key opportunities that you could develop? What are the threats that challenge your business venture or career opportunity?

Let us say you have decided to set up a student enterprise networking club. What do you have to offer that will help develop the project. Do you have contacts which will help? Have you any marketing background or access to finance?

What weaknesses do you have as a recent graduate? Is there something missing? Do you have the clout to make things happen? Have you experience of running one before? Do you have the management skills?

Is there a clear opportunity now? Is the opportunity local or is it nationwide? Is the opportunity a good profit model or should it be a social enterprise?

What threats are there? Is there a similar organisation that people can join? What specific risk financial or otherwise does the project have?

*Task 2*

Do a SWOT analysis of yourself in relation to your business or career objectives. What does your SWOT analysis tell you?

## Unique Selling Proposition

What is your USP or Unique Selling proposition? What do you offer that nobody else does? What is your competitive advantage? What separates you from any other competitors?

*Product*

What is your product? What are you actually offering? What service product or information are you offering the market place? What exactly will you do? What is your proposition in one sentence?

*Price?*

How do you price yourself on the market? What are you worth? What market are you after? Where are you positioning yourself? The price is a key component. How have you worked out your price? Are you prepared to hold out for it? Are you a £50/day £500 or £2000/day person?

*Place*

How are you going to operate? Is this going to be within a company or as a business? Where will you reach your client? Will you make use of modern technology? How international is your product or service? What is your distribution system? How will people access you either within the company or in the world? Have you the capacity to reach out to the emerging markets in India and China?

*Promotion*

It is important to have a good marketing mix. Your product, price and place must be in line with what the market has shown it needs. However in marketing yourself once you have identified who and where your customer is you create your offering to suit the market. The key part of the marketing mix is to make your market aware that you are available and appropriate for marketing needs. In some cases this may lead directly to sales but in many cases you and key advisers may need to use personal influence to close the deals that good promotional activity will cause.

We are all a little bit uneasy as to how celebrities continually promote themselves or the lengths that those who fall off the ladder will go to get back in there. However if you want to make that business work, get that job and continue to get opportunities you need to first of all be comfortable with the concept of self promotion. It would be nice if your good work was enough to ensure you got the results you required, but even in traditional professions today there is the recognition that you need to make other people aware of what you do and promote your brand.

### Guerilla Marketing

It would be nice to have a huge marketing budget but you will have to adopt the same strategy as many small businesses. You will have to be a "Guerrilla Marketer" that is adopt promotional strategies that produce maximum results with minimum expenses. The key is maximum publicity and awareness.

### PR

People do believe what they read in newspapers and magazine articles in newspapers will be read. Newsworthy material will be published. Newspapers and magazines are always looking for interesting material.

You also need to look for opportunities to make the news. It is all about building a relationship either directly or indirectly through a PR consultant.

### Networking

You need to harness the power of positive word of mouth. Join networks that will help you meet people who are eminent in your field. You need to have a system to make contacts and also to keep in touch with them. A network almost has a financial worth. Some people in your network will know people who know people who will be able to explain or help with key areas which could prove of use to your business or career. Again, it may not cost money directly but you need to work for it. It requires effort, planning and organisation. If you go to a networking event you should have set goals, review your performance and have a systematic way of keeping in touch with new contacts.

The key thing in personal marketing is that you want to use the power of word of mouth marketing. Networks are only one of a number of methods which could prove effective in getting the geometric progression available from word of mouth marketing. What will get your profile out there.?

Look at workshops, seminars the internet and any other way to deliver word of mouth marketing.

The key lesson is you can't sit and wait for positive word or mouth marketing to work. You must positively influence the process and make sure that the most powerful tools are used.

## Market Segment

Which market segment are you after? You can divide your potential customer group up accordingly to various factors including income, gender and region. You need to decide which segments you are after and why. Say you target all small businesses with less than 5 employees you must be sure that this will meet your strategic purposes. They are unlikely to have a budget to fund growth consulting or a high level job. However involvement will give real responsibility and opportunity to make a difference.

### Task

You decide you want to be a sales consultant for a pet products business. Divide up the possible market segments; decide which one to go after and why.

Market segmentation is important because your message needs to be answered clearly at one or two groups. You are likely to be less focused if your market is "everyone". Ideally as a business person it is good to find a niche where your experience and resources will leverage high results.

## Packaging

How are you packaging yourself and your work? Individually they can include dress and personal appearance. It can also include how services are laid out, how your portfolio will appear.

## Market Research

As mentioned earlier clever ongoing use of market information should lead to strategic shifts of marketing mix activities where this proves necessary.

## Product Enhancement

You should be continuously trying to improve your knowledge, qualifications, and experience to enhance the "product" which in this case is you.

## Branding

It is important you develop a brand which people recognise and to try to encourage customer loyalty. As part of the brand image you will have to consider the packaging appeal.

## Product Life Cycle

For your business or your career you should analyse where it is in the product life cycle. For instance if you are opening a sandwich bar, this is not a new concept unless you have some very innovative features. If you were deciding to become a celebrity through the power of "reality TV". You would at this stage have to be very careful as to how you would use this vehicle. Many of the programmes are now flagging. Ironically a few of the business programmes are still at an early stage of their lifecycle and would therefore be a better vehicle. You will need to come up with new strategies or markets for products reaching saturation point and will need a very effective guerrilla marketing system if you are at an early stage and are looking at a pioneering role. There is a lot of hard work to do before proof of concept. Let us say you want to be England's first professional bullfighter this idea would be at an early stage and you would have to adopt your marketing ideas appropriately.

### Price

Your price will be affected by demand, to put it bluntly. You want to be a trainee lawyer. There are loads of law graduates looking for the places, so the legal firms can keep salaries down. The key question when looking at your business product is where do you see the pricing going in the long run, and what is your strategy to get there?

### Advertising

You need to always be wary of advertising which has to be targeted and product measurable results. To create brand awareness you will get much greater impact by using more subtle methods, for instance a newspaper column which could promote you as an expert.

Ideally any form of promotion should be considered which could produce results. You must find out what works best and does not have strategic advantages. Particularly with professions there is a perception that the professional that has to advertise for work must not be any good. That is fine and dandy but how do you get work when you put that nameplate up and don't have a list of NHS customers? You need to promote not only to get business but to get the type of work you are looking for in the long run.

You may want work done but have a very specific long term strategic vision. It can be hard to satisfy this in the long run.

Let us say if you want to work long term in an Investment bank but need to short term get a job in financial services. Where possible you promote yourself to a market segment that will have some type of link however tenuous with investment banking. Interestingly enough many people have difficulty thinking strategically.

Whatever media you use you need to be clear what you want to achieve. One graduate started out as an architect had the simple strategy to get as much work as possible and promoted everywhere effective but getting lots of small jobs and a reputation as "the cheapest in town". Two years later he found himself with lots of small work at a low margin and with not even the time to think of the large building contractor market he was aiming for. He had to sell that practice and completely "rebrand" himself.

It is also hopefully obvious that you need to use a media which will reach your target audience. It may please friends and family to see your article in your local paper on your stockbroking expertise in London. Much more effective would be something read by people in the profession or were looking to invest significant sums with a stock broker in your area.

## AIDA

This should always be the underlying design model for any promotional activity you undertake.

| | | |
|---|---|---|
| A – | Attention | make the customer aware |
| I – | Interest | attract their interest |
| D – | Deal | get them to deal with you |
| A – | Action | get them to take some action steps |

*Task*

You are a newly qualified chartered surveyor and want to promote your career in commercial property in London. What 3 things can you do to make it happen?

## Other Promotional Activities

You can also use free samples point of sale displays competitions or other numerous promotional techniques. Again it has to be suitable for you. Are you building a database? How can you get people to use the product or service even once?

For those of you who have a service, you don't quite have to go to the extent of the actor Claude Van Damme who did high kicks outside a restaurant where a Hollywood producer always dined.

However you get the idea. Find a way for a large company or customer to sample your services without any obligation.

The type of promotion does depend on

(a) the stage of the product life cycle has been reached
(b) the nature of the product itself
(c) if you have any budget
(d) the nature of the target market.

Do you need to be known locally or internationally?

## Public Relations

As well as using the media you can also give services or products "pro bono" and create awareness. It is vital you are also committed to the charitable cause also otherwise it can very easily turn to negative public relation. Celebrities have learnt to their cost that agreeing to work with a charity for profile and then maybe cancelling engagements in favour of more commercial opportunities can be left with negative public relations profiles.

Remember though you are a brand, you may not be under media scrutiny like the Beckhams but everything you do counts. If you are promoting an image as someone who supports family values, living the life of a playboy tends to place you in the position of being a hypocrite.

However the person who is clever at personal marketing will try to use whatever their competitive advantage is and indeed whatever situation they find themselves in whatever the problem.

### Watch How Other People Market Themselves?

Watch someone who is building a professional reputation or someone who is building a celebrity profile. What steps do they take? Watch how they try to keep their profile up. We do love to see the celebs particularly the D list who have slipped from say the B list, and will do literally anything on TV to get their profile back. We enjoy it, particularly if it doesn't work.

However you can learn lessons. Celebs will spend at least 25% of their time promoting their profile. You need to invest at least 10% of your time no matter how busy you are at present in marketing yourself and keeping your profile up. If you have one major customer or employer who is paying you very well it is natural to think why bother? However fall out with that key source of income and suddenly you are in difficulty without the income or career profile that will help your marketing activities. That is why there is the old truism from careers advisers "It is easier to get a job when you have one".

I constantly see some students who attend business events in their holidays to make contacts have fun and search for future opportunities. I see lots of others who can't be bothered and are "too busy" to explore these opportunities. Obviously I hope you are different if you have taken the time and effort to read this book.

## Cross Fertilisation

You can be enterprising if you apply business practices which work in one industry to another. For instance if you have worked in the highly competitive world of financial services where marketing is a key element and you go to work for a firm of architects who do not know marketing. Adapting one of the marketing strategies from financial services could be highly innovative and profitable for the architectural practice.

## The Benefit of Varied Approaches

Like depending on one client depending on one personal marketing strategy is not enough. I saw one young accountant who built his practice on taking start up seminars for small business start ups for local enterprise agencies. He got lots of business. There were two problems with this. Firstly although he got lots of business, he was not getting established business and secondly when the enterprise agencies started to take the sessions themselves to save money he had no alternative strategy. Different activities can help each other provided they are part of a coordinated plan. They open up your services to a wider variety of sources and each method of marketing will impact the other.

## Your Personal Brand

Remember that you are a brand and that everything counts. This includes not only your activities but also everything from your posture, voice, tonality and small talk can make a difference. Like me you might get a shock if you were videoed to show how you come over. We would all prefer not to watch these films, but as you can imagine if you can relax you will learn a lot. It is very difficult otherwise to see and hear how we appear to others when presenting out personal brand.

## Online

Something you have to accept is that although "dot coms" are not necessarily always the favourite mode of business these days that you must make sure that your online profile matches up with the brand, the marketing message you want to present.

I learnt this lesson in an interesting way. My ten year old son bored at school decided to "Google" his father. Sounds like a painful process but as the modern techno kid that he is, he likes to use all available resources and gadgetry.

When I was "Googled" that is looked up, he found me at my place of work but found a very limited non existent profile. Whose fault was this? None other than my own.

If someone was considering doing business with myself or an associated company, one of the first things they would do is to use the power of internet to check up on my profile and any other evidence.

Marketing practitioners reckon that as part of your personal marketing agenda you should be very careful with your marketing information. On the internet as everything you do in your use of it, your membership of online communities and participation will all play a significant part in your marketing efforts, certainly in the strategic sense as this becomes more an more important. As we have already discussed word of mouth is very important and internet activity handled properly gives you the opportunity to reach out worldwide with your "blagging". Branding is very much about the image that people have of you. It is sensible not to ultimately get too worried and expect everyone to like you. However if you want to achieve significant career or commercial success you need to have more control of what the public perception is. The key question to ask yourself is do the right people notice what I do? If no you need to take corrective action. If you don't care, fine, but accept that the right people are those who will make the key commercial decisions. Yes if you do good work you deserve results but sadly that is not how it always works. Other people need to hear what you have done.

As part of your personal branding try to be more interesting, focus on the activities that will get results. If there is a forum where you can let other people know what you have done for instance like a company newsletter, let them know. They will always be searching for newsworthy items. If there is an opportunity to speak your mind do so. As we have said elsewhere you will always be communicating something, make sure it is the message you want to convey.

## Opportunity

To stand out you or your company need to be different. You need to see things differently, that is why creativity and seeing different angles can be important. Many times you have to work with both yourself and what you do now and use that to find a breakthrough to do different things. Being enterprising is all about open mindedness and being prepared to take action to do something. Again as suggested in the creativity session sometimes the new solution will come from looking at an industry or area that you have never considered before.

Again you are marketing yourself to an outside work and have always got to make the best use of your time and effort. I do think a range of activities is important but sometimes you will find a key opportunity which will provide an opportunity to maximise your profile.

## Where Are You Now?

As you know I recommend that you do try to measure where you are now. It is like the example I gave where I noticed that I was not paying enough attention to my online profile.

Do something about it. It could be a shock for you to realise that your profile is not out there. Do something about it. Can you in one or two sentences explain exactly what you do for your employer or customer, what benefit you provide and what is your unique selling proposition. You must then get that message out, in whatever your "guerrilla marketing" strategy is, and be flexible along the way never losing focus what the end objective is. Running about at breakneck speed will not necessarily achieve anything if you have not planned and ensure that all you effort is geared to the right audience at the right time with the right message.

### Relationship Marketing

People are very wary of those who suddenly become their best friend to achieve a marketing objective and then disappear until they need something again. A lot of your long term marketing benefit will come from people you deal with time and again who trust you.

### Who Are You Focusing On?

I am trying to get you to work on your self promotion; however I must also urge you to do this with the focus of others. Are you constantly trying to give your audience/clients what they want? You may need to demonstrate clearly you have done it but really making the marketing philosophy part of your belief system will pay dividends.

It is obvious if you have your own business to take this focus, but if you work within an organisation it is important to think go all the people you are working with. Why are they dealing with you? What result are they looking for? And what impact can your activities have? Could you do anything more to make a greater contribution?

If you want to do work for a new customer? Find an opportunity to d something on a small scale to demonstrate your worth.

### Always Deliver

Whatever marketing activity you can undertake, whoever you are marketing to, one of the key messages is that you will always deliver what you promise. This will shock people as it turns the normal strategy of "over promise/under deliver" on its head.

## Learn from Companies

Look at how major brands achieve success – What is it about NIKE or McDonalds etc that make you want to use them, rather than the opposition? How can you use this in your own case? What strategies worked and might work in a different setting?

## Testing

You may not be a business but it is always important to test what is working. Where is the profile coming from? What are you getting out of it? You need to track responses but also the difference between people who have noticed, and those who have as a result of your marketing have actively engaged with you.

The whole concept of personal marketing is not just to get some recognition of you as a brand but we also want tangible results. Following ParetosLaw (a favourite of mine I know) 20% of your activities will yield 80% of the results, and you have to increase these priorities.

Look at the different events that can yield your results. They may be presentations, e-mails, your attendance at returning events, your online profile/– which is working? Can you change your approach a little in each and measure the result? Small changes can be the levering point to lead to overall significant improvement. The ability to break down each process and measure the changes are good.

### Task

How do you market itself? Break down the process. Set up a system to measure the performance of each.

## Endorsement

The endorsement of key influencers will always play a significant part.

### Relationships

Systematically build relationships with other people and organisations where you will actively seek information and help each other. Always try to contribute to other people you want to work with even before a deal is struck. You need to formally look for referrals or chances to do interesting projects. Always be willing to help anyone within your organisation with new projects.

If you own a business you are attempting to find the ideal customer who needs the benefits that your products or services can bring. The clarity in knowing the end customer, their needs and what particular problems they have are vital before system design. The same applies internally within an organisation or a community. Who could be a key influencer in your career and what could you contribute to help them with their performance?

When someone is running a business most people can accept the need for a formalised referral process. Some will feel this is seen as a manipulative process by some in the corporate world new to "office politics". I have often sympathised with this viewpoint however we are talking about you achieving your goals and being the best you can be. If you leave things to chance there will be no correlation between your performance and your rewards. If you refuse to personally market yourself you are not making other people aware of what you can do and be given an opportunity to work with them. It is up to you.

### Clients or Contacts You Have Lost

You will find out the hard way in business. You will have disagreements with people both internally and externally no matter how good your intentions. The key is as part of your marketing agenda is to part as amicably as possible and to keep in touch. You, your position, or circumstances may have changed so it could be useful to get in touch again and try to rebuild the relationship. If you have not already dealt with the cause of the disagreement, now is the time to do so.

### Other Promotional Tools

How do you keep people informed as to what you are up to now?

Direct mail and or email in an organised fashion can keep you in touch with your client base.

### Use the Internet

Use the internet to target the key prospects.

### Go Through Your Contacts

Sit down and go through your contacts, internal and external. Divide them into appropriate categories. You want to find the people who either themselves or who know people who need benefits you can offer. You are trying to find trends or connections to be as efficient as you can. The big thing in personal marketing is that you do not have the time or resources to launch a major full time marketing campaign. However you must apply Paretos law and get the 80% of results that 20% of your time can identify. Decide also what is the best strategy to use. It may well be a short email or written note should be followed by a phone call. As someone who uses email extensively I know you must guard against the tonality of your emails.

There will be many cases where the phone call and the face to face meeting are the only way to make things happen.

### Your Own Website

There was a time as with all aspects of the internet where every small business had a website and every individual had one. I am not saying that it is strictly necessary in every case but with good marketing strategy to drive either the internal traffic on an intranet or outside traffic websites do have a significant part to play in your marketing. The creation of a virtual community with similar interests to you not only yields potential/profitable but also provides research advice and ongoing learning. The use of search engines and possibly a number of sites for each niche can be considered.

A small company I know has 24 different websites aimed at 24 different niches.

The other key potential is that you can reach out on a global basis without necessary leaving your office. Potential business from the new emerging, economies can be obtained that way.

## Create a Marketing Budget

If you have little money available to invest in your marketing it could be useful to offer some of your products/services in return for marketing help.

### Task

Make a list of all the products/services your company offers. Make a list of the people you deal with. Make a list of external stakeholders. Can you see any connections between the lists? Any communication lines that need to be set up? List any other stakeholders you would like to add to the list.

## Keeping in Contact

You can see there are so many things to do. How do you maintain contact with all these people? You need to keep communication with people who are important to you. The type of communication is also important. Some of you will be calling this chapter "the how great thou art" chapter as I seem to be advising you to "blow your own trumpet". I am certainly advising you to make others aware of your achievements. Ongoing communication with contacts need to be looking if possible at their interests, maintaining the marketing focus. Can you imagine how people would react if you were following up on sales to see if they were getting the result you promised?

What you need to do is once you have done your list is to set up a simple system that will allow you to stay in touch. You and anyone who helps have to do this with sincerity otherwise it is so easy to lose touch with people as you are too busy getting on with the business.

## A Marketing Plan

You need a plan with a set of goals and measurable events towards the end product. Again it is what you do on a weekly basis rather than once a year which will determine whether your marketing strategies are a success. It is too easy if things are going well with one strategy or if you are too busy not to work systematically. However that forms the basis of your work, your feedback and marketing strategies. Whether you work for a company or run your own company marketing is a key life skill. It will decide ultimately how successful your career or business is. Devote at least 3 hours per week to marketing, much more if you are in business. It may not seem important. I remember as a businessman trying to set up one afternoon a week for marketing. This was a strategic move and I ought to be congratulated. However I didn't do it as I had so much work on and as "time is money" I wanted to invoice as much as possible. I came to regret it because the positioning of yourself, your company is up to you. Sometimes people are lucky without any strategy, but run into problems when there needs to be change.

Above all realise you do have a lot to offer. How can you do more? How can you reach more people or make an impact? Use marketing to help as many people as possible and be the best you can be.

### Task

Make one final plan on one page only. Who is your market? What benefits do they need? How will you reach them? How will you use marketing on an ongoing basis?

**Marketing is for life!**

# 5

# FINANCE

## FINANCE

### "Show Me the Money"

Money makes the world go around and I want to convince you to take it seriously. People either are obsessed by money or completely disregard it. This is not helped by the fact that up until now there has been virtually no money education in schools and at University only students who study it are bamboozled with a mix of complex formulae and jargon which sends them off to sleep and lack of understanding. I have found Chief Executives who cry when they have to look at a financial report and have met Accountants and Bank Managers who have no idea how to build wealth.

Whatever your motivation do not underestimate money. I do not want to turn you into a modern day scrooge who despite vast wealth makes no contribution and lives a miserable existence. Ebenezer still exists you know. I met one multi millionaire five years ago who was being sued by a 65 year old who had worked for him for twenty years as a van driver being paid £1-20 an hour. When I asked the old gent why he was bringing the case he explained. Last year after nineteen years of employment his boss head told him he was buying him Christmas dinner for the first time. Touched by this kind gesture he noticed something has been posted through his letter box at his house. When he opened the door there was a chick leg wrapped up in tin foil. His Christmas dinner! Needless to say he wasn't impressed and sued.

However money does play a significant part even if you are involved in an organisation which does not have the profit motive.

Community organisations spend their time starved of resources and public sector organisations now have to be accountable financially.

Many people have a phobia about money, accounts and anything to do with numbers. Usually it starts with difficulty with Maths at School and the creation of a fundamental belief "I hate numbers, I'm crap at Maths and will never be able to handle money"!

I do find it hard to understand the distinction at times as much of maths consists of algebra, geometry and various other areas which go beyond the ability to add up with a calculator. That is all you have to learn to do, maybe some multiplication and I promise you will have a greater understanding of money and the part it will play in your life. What is important is not only that you understand the part it plays in business/community ventures, but also what your financial aims are.

### The Realities

The reality is that you will spend a substantial part of your life working to either make or earn money to fund your life working to either make or earn money to fund your life and that of your loved ones and to provide for your retirement.

Those of you at University level may feel that money does not matter and that community issues and doing what you enjoy is all that is important. This may be disputed to many of you living in to-day's financial climate for students where student loans and part time jobs are the norm. Your parents may be trying to encourage you to finish off your training as a chartered surveyor when all you want to do is to travel, to maybe go and work on a Kibbutz in Israel. The last thing I want to do is to "rain on your parade" and travel and freedom are great at any stage. What I want is to make your decisions with an understanding of money and what the future holds.

### Do I Want Wealth?

I do recognise that your priorities will change, but it is important to think where you want to end up. That interesting post in the civil service may appear attractive now after years of student penny pinching, but there is one thing for sure, you will never be wealthy. Public sector jobs do offer index linked pensions and challenging work, but these are not a path to financial independence. The worst thing is that the person who is happy to get a public sector job now may well evolve into someone – who in ten or fifteen years time realises they wanted a different financial reality. Maybe you can leave and set up your own business but the odds are against you with years of pubic sector working and a secure job, and the commitments you will probably have gathered up.

Please do not misunderstand me. I want you to try to make a strategic decision and go into the world of work with your eyes open.

If wealth is something you would like to have, private enterprise is the best chance. Certain professions are also more likely than others to provide significant income opportunities, though most will more likely to lead to financial comfort rather than wealth and financial freedom.

Dentists, Doctors, Lawyers and Accountants are amongst those who should do comfortably. One local businesswoman I know who has six daughters, all went into investment banking a very lucrative sector as far as the world of employment goes.

Parental values I do understand as one myself. You want your child to have an enjoyable and worthwhile career as you have had yourself. You don't want your child to face the uncertainty of self employment and Entrepreneurship. You notice that the local dentist or lawyer tend to live in the bigger houses, drive the BMW's and have a good lifestyle. You then subtly encourage little Johnnie to go down that path. Forgive us our intentions are good but based on certain fake premises.

## Do What You Love

If you genuinely like something you will show lots of interest and take extra care in your work. Normally this will lead to excellent performance.

I do subscribe to a certain extent to the dictate "do, what you love and the money will follow". If you choose psychology as your area to specialise in this is not recognised as highly in the "parental professional" status file. However if you are a very good psychologist with some of the E Factor Skills outlined here particularly personal marketing you can do very well. However this is where an understanding of business/finance matters because you can easily take a different road. Many of the psychology jobs available are in the public sector and if you have you do not take an enterprising approach to your career development you an easily end up in a situation which only the most enterprising or innovative will escape. The brilliant psychology graduate at 21 can end up at 36 married with two children, an educational psychologist for the civil service all because of the initial route he or she chose. Please don't think I am demeaning this path, I just want you to make career and business decisions based on your long term financial values and goals. So do what you love but make sure you are enterprising enough to know where you want to end up and to consider taking options which open up possibilities at a later date.

The same applies to companies. If you are a mechanical engineer and you spend the first ten years of your career in the cigarette manufacturing industry you may well become an expert in cigarette machinery. This is not transferable to other industries and you have committed your career to what is essentially a declining industry due to worldwide trends.

### Employment or Self Employment

I want you to be as enterprising as possible. Therefore I should be recommending self employment. However there are advantages and disadvantages. Employment with a large multinational will offer a lot of benefits that self employment or employment with a community office cannot.

You know exactly where you are financially and can therefore plan more easily for savings mortgages etc. However you will pay PAYE which means tax and National Insurance will be deducted from your gross pay at source with very little room for expenses or allowances. This means that as regards net income you will be better off earning the same gross fees as a self employed person. What I do advise you to do whether as a self employed person, see yourself as a "provider of Services" even if you are an employee and make sure you are getting the best possible return both financially and in terms of career prospects and professional development.

Having attended a recent Scottish institute of enterprise conference I was pleased to see that a number of major corporation employers are actually looking for employees with the Enterprise Skills that form part of the E-Factor.

In making your career decision at this stage look at where the long term career path with the organisation can lead financially.

It is difficult for you to assess at this stage. A managing director earning £150,000 for a major company can seem like a dream, when you have just finished your daily shift at McDonalds at £4.15 per hour. However remember it costs £750,000 to buy a decent house in London and as an employee your £180,000 is approximately £75,000 net, £6000 a month. Add a couple of kids and a spouse at home the 70hrs a week the job demands is not quite as attractive as it first appears.

However for the Enterprisers if the company has a good training programme and offers significant early opportunities for training and responsibility it is a chance to learn some of your mistakes as part of your experience. I am all for "the school of hard knocks" but too many too early in your career could put you out of the running for a long time.

### Self Employment

I am one of those people whose mission is to encourage other people in particular graduates to start their own business particularly Global Business. However I want to focus on the financial advantages and disadvantages of self employment. Having done that I will give you a strategy which will boost the finances of both parties whatever route you choose.

### Financial Advantages of Self Employment

One of the biggest advantages are the tax implications. A self employed person is able to claim a much greater range of expenses against their taxable income. Let us compare the case of a chartered surveyor earning gross income of £50,000 and compare their situation as employed or self employed. The employee will pay approximately 50% of their income as tax and national insurance. Not only does the self employed person pay virtually no national insurance saving almost £5000: They suddenly are able to claim as deductible all sorts of expenses. The running costs of the car used, travel, wife's wages if she helps with the business, going to exhibitions indeed anything which could be related to pursuing the business knock off say in net tax terms up to another £5000. Quite significant!! Now its not always this straightforward but there is a significant tax advantage.

### Other Advantages

There is also no cap on your income. You charge what you are worth. You are only limited by the time you can spend and what your client will pay. There is no limit to this if your business is providing information or products. You also can hopefully make money off people who work for you.

### Disadvantages

There are the key self employed financial disadvantages. Firstly cash flow. Your ability to pay your bills and reinvest can be determined by when your clients pay you. If you are lucky enough to run a cash business, it is accepted practice to pay for your coffee or your beer at the point of purchase. Once the standard procedure is invoicing to a certain extent you are at the mercy of the company who owes you money. If they are a large company and decide not to pay you for a couple of months, there is probably not a lot you can do despite government late payment legislation. Meanwhile you may be relying on your bank manager to help you pay your creditors unless your creditors will give you a similar payment time period to your customers.

### Risk

The other key financial indicator is risk. You do risk financial failure in running your own enterprise. You will operate an uncertain environment. Arguably though this exists in large companies namely even in traditionally safe sectors such as Banking or Teaching.

## Conclusion

Whether you are ready to run your own enterprise is up to you. There is lots of support there and to be honest you can cut down your personal risk with limited company status (see streetwise guide, Dave Marshall Ryan)

However some of the enterprise skills I am trying to teach you in this book will be learned more effectively in running your own business.

There are various half way house solutions. Start a part time enterprise as long as it is not against the regulations of your employer, create a tax loss and set it against your paye tax.

Sign up for any type of experiential learning which aims to allow you to do things, experience the rollercoaster of business in a safe environment. An example of this is the tv reality show "The Apprentice" where the contestants get a lot of chance to put into practice the skills we are talking about here. There is no doubt that there is nothing like the real thing. I am not saying you have got to set up a large business and take all the risks, but a venture even part time will yield a lot of the lessons and make you "streetwise". What is important is that you treat community as well as business ventures as financial challenges and learn the financial reality through your experiences. Also be clever enough to learn from both successful and unsuccessful business people. If I was going to give you another enterprise skill it would be to continuously learn.

You will make mistakes, learn from them and don't make the same mistakes again.

So lets continue finance.

101 If you can make these part of your behaviours this will serve you well wherever you end up.

*Task*

Have a go at setting out your financial goals. What would you like to be earning in a year, five years, ten years? What type of lifestyle would you like to lead?

## Business Finance

Handling money in your own venture demands certain skills/disciplines because of the uncertainty and risk of business. Get the fundamentals right and it will help your chance to make your enterprises work and is also very applicable to apply to corporate/community ventures and indeed to your personal finances.

## Cash is King

Cash flow dictates the survival of a business as opposed to profit. You can be making money on paper but if it is not there when you have to pay certain bills you are potentially insolvent at that moment.

Let me illustrate this – you are running your own business, for the past three months. Your sales are £1,000 month 1, £2,000 month 2 and £3000 month 3 – and you have to pay expenses of £1500 every month. Even though your sales are £6000 and expenses £4500, you

are going to have cash flow problems, because you are paid two
months behind.

| Month 1 | Month 2 | Month 3 |
|---|---|---|
| Cash In NIL | O/B (1500) | O/B (3000) |
| | | Cash In 1000 |
| Cash out (1500) | Cash in NIL | Out (1500) |
| Bank (1500) | Cash out (1500) | (500) |
| | C/B (3000) | C/B (3500) |

The business will gradually catch up as your sales are more than expenses but at the moment you can't pay your bills without the help
of the bank.

That is why planning your financial budget is important but particularly for businesses, so you can cover the periods that cash flow
will be slow. You have also got to be tough at credit control getting
paid as soon as possible.

All businesses/organisations pay a lot of bills. If they think you are
quite relaxed about getting paid guess what you go to the back of the
queue!!

Spell out your credit terms and adopt a fair but firm policy. Otherwise even when you are making money it will be in your creditors
bank account.

### Task 2

Look at your financial budget for the next 6 months. Are you sure
enough is coming in to meet outgoings. How can you plan for this?

## Profit

Although cash flow is vital to keep bills paid it is important to realise
that you are in business to make a profit, and even as a community
or public sector organisation you do not want a deficit and want to at
least break even.

Believe it or not you can get so busy doing the work and running an operation that you will lose track as to why you are in business.

Stuart Wilde an author on spiritual enlightenment launched a worldwide business a number of years ago. As you can imagine the people who ran his companies were more interested in their karma or spirituality rather than the performance of the business. Like Stuart they wanted to save the world but he gradually realised his business was not performing.

Stuart Wilde hit on a novel way of letting his managers understand the realities of business. After enduring phone calls for a month about how much they were enjoying their meditation sessions and how good they felt their karma was Stuart used a different strategy to shake them up.

He would ring them every day once a day and ask "how many, how much?", and then slam the phone down. After two weeks they got the message. Stuart wanted to know how many books they were selling each day, and how much their turnover was. The business changed their attitude changed. They still wanted to save the world but they knew they had to make the business viable to do this. If you are in business no matter what contribution you make you are in it to make and collect the money. There is no other reason to be in business other than this. Lose sight of this and you will be in trouble.

Even in community or public sector organisations you may not have the profit motive but you are judged on the efficiency of your operation and future funding and budgets depend on this. I still don't want you to make money your goal but you have got to operate within financial constraints and handle money or it will handle you!!

### Pricing Margin

Get your pricing right and control your costs in line with this margin and volume are key variables in whether a venture will work or not. Ideally you want as good a margin as you can get. You also need to ensure you are still getting the appropriate margin and or return on your time. You should only sacrifice margin for a large enough volume of work.

Whether you are running your own business or working for a company you should always measure the return you are getting for the effort put in. Remember self employed or employed you are giving your skills for an adequate return. Every hour you spend working is an hour with an opportunity lost.

So get the appropriate price. As a business you need to remember that you have to recover both direct and indirect costs. Pricing is also a psychological area. How much do you value yourself and your contribution/product. There is no point quoting a price of £1000 per day for your work for a community budget with a maximum budget of £500 per day. However perhaps you should contribute in another way or work in another market where there are financial rewards appropriate for your contribution.

Particularly with personal services there is an element of what you charge is the worth you attribute to yourself. I am sad to disillusion you but the old truism that if you don't value yourself, nobody else will. If you will sell your services for a cup of coffee, that is all the other party will offer.

## The Bottom Line

"The bottom line is relentless"

Gaining some financial knowledge will help you make decisions. You must be sure you are getting your profit margins or in a community project to meeting the financial criteria set.

## Income Should Exceed Expenditure Go!

You have always to act according to your means. It is important to dress well and act the part of where you want to end up, but not if it involves taking on massive financial commitments you are not ready for. For instance you feel you need to drive a 7 series BMW at £600 a month leasing as a trainee architect on £10,000 a year.

### Keeping Your Head

Again if your small business starts to go well and you suddenly have money in the bank or have got a substantial salary increase. This is your defining moment. Can you do a Rudyard Kipling and "treat triumph and disaster just the same". It goes without saying that keeping a cool head when you are in financial difficulty is important and obvious. Equally hard though is keeping your head when things seem to be taking off. With self employment in particular even if your own business is riding high at present there is no guarantee that it will be in the next calendar year. You will also be liable to pay approximately 1/3 rd of your ill gotten gains to the taxman at the end of the year put some aside, retain some for tax and by all means enjoy some of it.

### Financial Documents

We have already talked about cash flow, profit and balance sheets. It is important that you understand what these documents mean if you are either a would be or an actual Entrepreneur. For enterprising corporate or community people to understand these documents will advance your career. Arguably using the documents as a tool for personal, financial planning can help you achieve your financial goals.

1.   Profit and Loss

Let us do a simple profit and loss for 1 year. Let's say you run a restaurant.

| | |
|---|---|
| Sales | 300,000 |
| Cost of Sales | 150,000 |
| Grass Profit | 150,000 |
| Running Expenses | <u>135,000</u> |
| Net profit | 15,000 |

The profit and loss measures your gross margin after the manufacture of your product and the net margin after all claimed expenses.

Your gross margins 150,000     gross profit
                 300,000     sales

= 50% Every time you spend 50p making and selling the product you make £1. The average for the restaurant industry.

Your net margin is    £15000     net profit
                £300,000     sales

=5% Every time you have £1 of sales you are claiming 5p. This document includes all sales whether paid or not and all running costs whether paid or not. So you can make a profit on paper – but if the cash flow is not right you can still be struggling.

The gross margin above is really a test of operational efficiency. The net margin reflects whether the overheads or running costs are in line with the net profit. Again whether in business or personal life it is very easy for costs to exceed income and in particular cash flow.

Money spent unnecessarily is opportunity missed for savings business and long term strategies. However I don't want you to turn out to be like a certain 70 year old multi millionaire I met recently who was almost in tears telling me he could now afford to go to Scotland due to Easyjets low airfares. I don't think he was getting the full benefit of his money.

## The Balance Sheet

The Balance sheet is another of those financial statements which you should know about whether as a business or individual. It is a snapshot of what you are worth at any one particular moment in time.

*Examples*

You are a forty year old male. You own your own house worth £200,000 and have £20,000 savings in the bank. You have a mortgage of £100,000.

Your Personal Balance Sheet as at today's date

Assets House  £200,000
Savings       £20,000
Total Assets  £220,000

Liabilities
Mortgage      £100,000
Net Worth     £120,000

The man has items worth money of £220,000 but owe £100,000 against this. He is worth after paying all his bills £120,000.

The key to long term financial success either as an individual or a business is to build a strong balance sheet. A pension is ultimately an asset, a sum of money from which eventually you can have an income or buy an asset such as a business property or other investment in time or money.

Some people are lucky to be given shareholdings in lucrative family businesses or property portfolios. For the rest of us it is necessary to build a portfolio of assets. For those of you particularly in the public sector or major corporate entity you will be focused on establishing a pension. Nothing wrong with that except in many cases due to the changes in population etc. there are not many schemes which offer a guaranteed excellent return. You should therefore think about building some assets for yourself to lessen your risk and give you a better return.

The danger of having a high powered job at say £100,000 a year, or a small business making you the same you are unlikely to build assets unless you set out to do so. With the job you will hopefully have some type of pension scheme the self employed will have a better net income due to tax advantages but if either party pretty much live a lifestyle which matches their income don't create a surplus which they use in an enterprising and innovative way you are likely to struggle financially in a long term basis.

## Task

Draw up your own balance sheet now. Be honest. It is not where you are now but where you are going to end up. Check it at least once per year. The better the balance sheet the greater freedom you have to do what you want. To increase it you have to be strategic something which is very hard when you are young and which can look pointless when you are old.

## Financial Strategy

Being strategic is looking beyond the next five years. To get where you want to be in the long term live for the moment but the decisions you make now will have consequences in the long run. Unfortunately both business and individuals seem to vary between the cost conscious scrooge type to the party animal who whatever he makes, spends more. Some people get confused as to how pop stars and celebrities or even business people who earn millions can end up with nothing. Simple they gross a million on which they owe say £400,000 tax. They party and spend £ the million and next year as can happen in any business they earn very little. The problem is they owe £400,000 tax, and have no money to pay it, and no money to sustain their new lifestyle. Before you think I am turning into a bore I do appreciate a quote attributed to George Best a former Northern Ireland Footballer who has made his way through a few millions in his time "I spent most of it on wine, women and parties. I wasted the rest", or the elderly porter in an Edinburgh hotel on bringing champagne to Bests room when he was staying playing matches for Hibernian; Best had won £10,000 in the casino and was sitting with ex Miss World Mary Stavi his girlfriend, "Mr Best Where did it all go wrong?"

The answer is to have a strategy. If you have a business try to re-invest a portion of the profits. The first person you should pay at least 10% is to yourself before you start to spend your daily living costs".

Also set aside 10% that you enjoy now on whatever you want.

I don't want you to become an accountant. I wouldn't recommend it. I believe you should be taking calculated risks and accountants like bank managers tend to be very good at analysing things tearing them apart and rejecting them. They often count the beans for the successful enterpriser/ E Factor person. However you should take on board their good qualities. When you are spending money it is good not to get too emotionally attached to material things, otherwise you will buy them when you can't afford them or pay too big a price for them. You see a flat that you want at £100,000 you have just started your first job. Your friend an Estate Agent says it is a good buy at £100,000 nothing more. The bidding goes up to £130,000 and you still try to buy it, you are "emotionally attached" to buying something at the wrong price.

## Cash Flow Forecasting/Budgeting

Not another financial document. I knew it he is trying to turn us into an accountant after all!

It is simply this is a good idea, particularly for a business, to plan ahead for income and expenditure and liken the cash is likely to come in and go out of the business. The timing of cash flow can play an important part. Sods law will dictate that all your major bills will become due when income is unlikely to be available for banking. If need be you need to arrange overdraft facilities to ensue you don't have a financial "met down" situation. This budget is often known as a business plan. You plan ahead and make sure you can deal with financial uncertainty.

If you are not keeping within the budget at an early stage you need to take corrective action to get back on track.

It is a bit late as a businessperson to realise you are having money problems because the bank is returning your cheques. Crucial for a business and still important as an individual. There are some simple software systems available that can roll out budgets based on entering a few statistics. Use it to keep track, enjoy yourself but without compromising your financial strategy.

Here is what a budget should look like. Don't be dazzled by the reems of figures. It is simply a list of your planned spending and income receipt over the period of Budget.

Jaynes Consultancy six month cash budget

|  | 1 | 2 | 3 | 4 | 5 | 6 |
|---|---|---|---|---|---|---|
| Income | 0 | 0 | 0 | 2000 | 3000 | 2000 |
| Expenditure |  |  |  |  |  |  |
| Costs | 1000 | 1000 | 1000 | 1000 | 1000 | 1000 |
| Salary | 1000 | 1000 | 1000 | 1000 | 1000 | 1000 |
|  |  |  |  |  |  |  |

*Task*

Does Jayne have a cash flow or profit/problem? Look at the figures, I will give you the answer on the next stage.

**Conclusion**

Money is only a resource to be used for you to develop a business and live your life to the fullest. Unfortunately many people are unable to handle money and it takes away from their enjoyment of life. What I am warning you is that unless you go and live in a cave, it is very difficult to avoid money. Let us say you despise business you want to do good and go and work for a charity for disabled people. As their manager what will be the first document you look at that will govern how you run the charity? Yes the budget. You have to live within your funding to keep the community work going. For me it is simply a tool which carefully used can enhance the contribution of your business and help you do what you want with your life. I know it is difficult, particularly, for those of you who may not need to think about it and have a simple solution to all financial issues in life. All I can say is handling money cleverly is part of the enterprising persons make up. They may look for specialist financial advice when required, but they usually consider the financial consequences of their decisions and make the right moves to get what they want. I quite respect those of you who unlike me refuse to contemplate becoming a millionaire. However money can play such a part in blocking business start up or growth. Many good people end up working forty hours a week just to live a fairly mundane life.

I feel if you have an enterprising/innovative capacity you should have a chance to apply this, live life and help others. Don't let the lack of key financial strategies hold you back!

**Raising Money**

Any enterprise business or community has to raise money to start up, grow or survive.

My belief is if the project is good enough there is money available for somewhere your job is to find it and persuade the funders to back you. This applies even if you work within a large company where senior managers will have to agree to include your project within their budgets.

In raising funds this is where your personal influence and marketing skills will help in building your financial acumen and results. You will quickly realise that not every one will agree to back you. For instance lets say you are opening a new juice bar in your local town. You have just graduated and you ask your local bank manager to lend you £5000 and he says no. For some people the rejection is a real blow and they give up on idea of starting their own business. The reality is as a young person with no capital and no assets for him to secure the loan against you are a bad risk. However if you research available information you will find there are specialist loan and grant schemes available to help people under 30 start their own business and a range of other options available.

## What Will Funders Want to Know?

They will want to see your business plan budget and why you need the money. However not only is the business model being evaluated, but also your ability to manage is under review. Will you stick at it? Will you sell and make it happen. ? So getting the funds can be very much selling exercise both on paper and in person.

ANSWER Jayne has initial cashflow problems which will turn around in month 3.

## Debt

There is good debt and bad debt. Loans, to buy a range of consumer goods are only to be recommended on a limited basis although some type of mortgage for property and a possible car loan are acceptable. Too much consumer debt can mean you have to work 40 hours a week simply to service your loans and credit card debt.

## Innovation Financing

Ideally you should always be looking for creativity in finding your funding for projects and personal ventures. Obviously it is a good idea to see if any grants are available as this is free money that does not have to be repaid. There are lots of funds available if you will search and look if you can meet their criteria.

## Private Investors

I am not recommending that you sell part of your family home to someone else, but in business ventures not enough enterprisers look for investment from outsiders. There are lots of outside "Business Angels" successful business people who want to invest money in venture with a possible long term return or even in community ventures which meet their strategic charity obligations.

## Leverage

I want to introduce you to the concept of "leverage". This is making money or achieving results using other peoples money, time or resources. It does sound like the original "capitalist" concept get the factors of production "work them into shape whatever the consequences and keep all the "filthy lucre yourself.

However it is not that. It is the time to have a few more reality checks.

Unless you are a pop star, famous sportsperson or a very exceptional Chief Executive there is a limit to what you can achieve in your own time. If you are going to set up a charity unless you are already wealthy you are going to have to use someone else's money to fund your project and the time of volunteers to make it happen.

Ideally in today's environment I would always recommend that you try to use leverage wherever you can. You have only a limited time and you do not want to work all the hours available just to get by because you have a private life, family and friends who need some of your time and you need to preserve a work/life balance to have the best possible life to cope with stress and to keep healthy.

It can be a quality of the enterprising person to want to do everything to make sure it is done. However using other resources can be much more effective.

It is why property can be such a good long term strategy. The Buy to Let market has become "overrated" and it may not necessarily be the perfect time to enter the market. However firstly property is an investment on which Banks will lend up to 85% of the funds. If the market is right and you get a tenant, their rental (other peoples money again) will pay the mortgage, provide cash flow and hopefully lead to capital gain, with very little of your input in terms of time.

It is also why you should carefully guard your ideas. If you have intellectual property such as a patent or copyright you may be able to get a financial return on its use.

I am suggesting you do this with the utmost integrity. There have been companies and politicians who have achieved wealth through the use of their countries resources, However use the leverage of others, ideally on a win win basis, or you will find that other people will be using your time to leverage their own projects wither in business or within an organisation.

## Taxes

Taxes can be a very substantial drain on building your wealth portfolio. However in most countries tax is the key collector of government income and it is the law that you pay your share. I am certainly not recommending evasion which is against the law. Tax avoidance where you plan your financial affairs to at least lessen tax liabilities needs to be considered. Let us say you have written a book and you have been offered £80,000. The book has take you five years to write and your probably won't write another one (don't worry ??? I will) This £80,000 one off lump sum could prove to be a substantial part of your investment portfolio and long term retirement income. It is perfectly reasonable to plan to limit your tax liability. For instance by operating within a company and making a substantial tax deductible self administered tax fund payment.

## Plan for Tax

If you are self employed you need to decide plan ahead for tax and get yourself the best deal without breaking the law. Limited companies can be very advantageous tax vehicles for growth businesses.

I don't want you to get obsessed about tax.

For employees there can be significant tax advantages in having a part time business which could claim expenses and provide potential tax rebate situations.

The important thing with tax is to be strategic. Before making any financial decision you should have a review with your tax adviser.

As an enterprising individual with financial skills you will always consider the tax angle as part of your decision.

However if you want to be based in UK or USA you will have some tax liability and need to accept that the most important thing financially is to make your margin and get paid. Getting used to setting aside 25% of the profits for tax provision is a good habit to get into.

## Ratios

One of the key areas any business person has to consider is ratios. These are a set of statistics based on financial statements. We have already talked about some of them, gross margin on sales net margin etc. If you can understand Balance sheets and profit you can measure the return on the worth of your business. Let us say your business balance sheet shows a bottom line figure of £100,000 but it only makes you £5000 a year that is not a good return on your investment.

In making decisions financially it depends on the ratios. If you buy a property for instance which may look very well or be in Spain your favourite holiday destination what is important is does the deal make sense. What did you pay against market value?

When you add up all the costs against the Return adjusted for periods without a tenant is it still a good deal? If it isn't walk away. Business is a numbers game. If you only look at one deal or one customer you tie yourself in. If you wanted to buy or start a business you should look at least 100 until you see the right business or right deal for you. The same applies to looking for a job.

## The Person You Are

The fascinating thing I found out by working in a bank or as an accountant is that it is the habits you have rather than your income which matter. You see people earning £60,000 per year and spending £62,000 and people earning £10,000 a year and saving £2,000 and buying commercial property.

You might dismiss this chapter as the ramblings of a boring accountant, (you may be right!). What I want to do is save you from some of the financial heartache I have experienced not because I didn't have financial qualifications, I became a qualified accountant and financial planner, but because having qualifications does not guarantee you have the competences and will act in the best way for yourself. A lot of the points I am making came from financial mistakes I made.

Be clear what you want to do financially. Do you want to be wealthy if so at what level? What lifestyle do you want? Have you the right plan to get what you want.

Like all the E Factors there is no better learning place than in the game of life. The next time you have a financial decision to make look at it differently.

My advice is to make money and use it wisely for your own freedom, your family and to help the community.

As one famous business person said "once you get money out of the way then you can be good". Get it out of the way by treating it with respect and have the strategies so that it helps you do what you want with your life.

We never found out what happened to the new scrooge in "A Christmas Carol" after he started treating people well and helping others. That did not make him a fool, but wealth and the ability to handle money whether as a business person or manager is a key requisite of the job and if you want to take part essential to enjoying your life in this commercial world.

Why don't you "show me the money" and complete the task to show you have got what it takes.

*Task*

Pick your own business or where you work. What will you have to do to be financially independent in 10 years? Email your plan. What financial changes do you need to make?

# 6

# INFLUENCE

## INFLUENCE

### Personal Influences

It is important to realise that none of your business career or life plans will come to fruition, unless you get other people to support your ideas. You need to convince other people that your ideas/projects will work and that you are the person to deliver them. So you need to influence/persuade others to back you. Influencing consists of a number of individual skills which we will examine, all of which are important in delivering results:

- Communication skills
- Networking skills
- Selling/negotiating skills

Unfortunately like many of the other enterprise skills, you are not taught these in any standard school or university course. However you can acquire them if you are prepared to learn the basic transferable skills but above all to apply and practice them in your every day life.

### Communication

Are you a good communicator? Other people need to be aware of your ideas/projects and you need to interact to make things happen. However there is more to communication than simply speaking or writing.

The fact is that you are always communicating whether you realise it or not. You communicate non verbally as well as verbally and unless you get it right you are unlikely to be as effective a communicator as you could be.

## Be a Listener

Ironically although we are trying to help you get better at getting your ideas across to persuade other people, one of the key skills is to genuinely take time to listen to other people as covey says "to understand before being understood".

I really don't mean pretending to be interested, I mean taking the time to understand where the other person is coming from, whether you agree with them or not. Everyone has a story to tell and a point to make. You will diffuse arguments, and have a better chance of persuading others if you can respect other people and their viewpoints.

Do it with sincerity or don't do it at all. I'm not saying that if you are at a party and you are cornered by the party "bore" you don't have to sit there in rapt attention for hours on end. However be interested in others and what they have got to say, you will never know what you might learn!!

Students, who go for management assessment job interviews with the large corporates, often try to get their point across to "boss" the group. What they don't realise is that the students who listen to others and understand where the group is going before they say anything are noticed. They are seen as having the best potential Why? Listening is a key skill. You need to understand your customer, friend, supplier or family member, and their priorities before you attempt to gain their support or influence.

Sincerity is everything both to learn and to communicate.

Now are you listening?

## Communication

You are constantly communicating whether you realise it or not. Communication is much more than just speaking or the written word. Your body language, your tonality, what you do, what you wear all communicates a message to others. We will discuss this again, when we talk about personal marketing.

## The Mix

Research has shown that Communication consists of 5% words, 40% body language and 55% tonality. People pick up on your non verbal communication does what you do, your body language and your tonality all give the same message?

For instance I met an old acquaintance this morning in a coffee shop. I asked him how he was and what he was doing. He said he was freelancing and looking about for the right position. However his flat tonality, lack of enthusiasm and poor posture/body move-ment told me he was in bad form and that things were not going too well. Am I a mind reader? Unfortunately not. I'm just saying that was the message he was giving me, unintentional or not. I could have put some work his way but the message I got was of someone in turmoil not ready to undertake some of the project work I needed done.

## Physiology

An Israeli psychologist believed that there was a strong link between mind/body, and that movement could improve your state. If you stood up straight, looked up and moved with greater energy, your mood would improve.

Try it!! Do you feel any better?

Let's say you are going in to meet your Bank Manager to seek funds for your new business, if you move confidently have good posture and give off a relaxed yet confident and business like de-meanour, he/she will take you more seriously. What they are trying to assess is does this person believe in this project, how they will react to pressure.? I do understand in going into this situation, it is easy to feel nervous and give off anything but positive vibes. However there is <u>a secret</u>. By moving your body as a confident person would you end up convincing yourself and feeling more confident, and ironically becoming the enterprising person the Bank Manager is looking for.

One Person who impressed me recently was a contestant on "Dragons Den" a recent television programme which focused on would be business people pitching their idea to a group of multimillionaires who are prepared to invest in their idea. This group usually start off by tearing the ideas and indeed the contests apart. This makes for compulsive viewing a bit like watching Christians being torn apart by lions in Ancient Rome.

However one very quiet young lady whose business consisted of fashion jewellery impressed me by both her ability to listen to the panels criticisms but also by her relaxed yet confident demeanour. She stood confidently, listened respectfully and responded not with aggression but with quiet confidence, again her voice, posture and words showing a quiet belief and a willingness to listen to other viewpoints.

The panel got the message, all respected her influencing skills and she got a major investor.

## Tonality

Tonality refers to more than just the pitch or timbre of your voice, important though that is it often represents the subtle message behind the words sound or written.

Many of us use emails or texts nowadays for quick communication. Sometimes communication by email only can deliver the wrong underlying message.

As you can imagine particularly in face to face discussions or over the phone, voice tonality can play a very important part. One of the key weaknesses many people have is lack of variety in their tonality,

vary it, make sure you put enthusiasm in your voice and that the tonality above all represents what you feel. You all know the feeling
that someone for instance has been "cool" to us over the phone, not
through the words used but by the tonality in the voice. Never underestimate the part it can play. Get it wrong and you can
significantly dilute the success of your communication. A potential
customer who you are asking to purchase from you stating "I believe
this product will increase your sales" will search for any sign that you
do not believe what you are saying. The voice tone can give that
message.

## Communication Styles

To communicate successfully the most important thing is to be flexible. Different styles of communication are appropriate for different
situations and for different people. Possibly the thing is to try to take
your time, assess what is appropriate and respond appropriately. You
may feel "I talk very enthusiastically and if they don't get the message
that is their fault".

However as part of your respect towards other people you need to
put over the message to the other party in a way that they will understand. As Richard Bandler a famous communication specialist has
said "the meaning of communication is the response you get". So the
responsibility is yours. Some people like "the big picture", some like
the detail. Your job as an influencer is to satisfy everyone.

## Sensory Systems

NLP one of the most popular communications models works on the
basis that everyone has a different view of the world. Some people
are visual, looking for visual evidence to understand everything,
some are auditory who like to hear things and some are into their
feelings and like to touch physical evidence.

They also use language related to their system. Visual people talk
about "getting the picture" Auditory like "the sound of things" and

for the kinaesthetic people things "feel right". Start listening to the language of people to see if you can identify what they prefer. Visual people often speak quickly in a high pitch voice and are obviously into how things look, including their physical appearance; auditory have great tonality in their voice and kinaesthetics speak slowly focusing on their feelings.

Very interesting you may say but so what? The danger is that if you are dealing with someone who has a different primary sensory system, the danger is if you are not aware you could be talking at different speeds and using different words. This is not likely to improve the communication process.

Let us say you are a feelings person presenting your findings on a project to your visual boss. You keep explaining how you have a good gut feeling about the project". You speak slowly and talk about "grasping the opportunity". Visual boss gets impatient with your slow rate of speech and interrupts and wants to know "what the big picture is". He comments that your Powerpoint slides are not colourful enough. Here you have a miscommunication.

What the good communicator does if they are making a speech is to work on visuals, 60%?? of the population, adding sounds, working on their speech and emphasis and giving out detailed handouts for the kinaesthetics to grasp. They use all three types of language, and if presenting to one key individual will do their best to use their preferred system. Are they being calculating, surely you should just be yourself and people should take you as they find you. NO that is haphazard, to communicate you need to get the message across and minimise the barriers to clear communication between both parties.

*Exercise*

Listen to the words people use. What is important to them? What do you notice?

## The Outcome Formula

With any communication be clear as to what outcome you want to achieve. Learn to carefully assess both verbal and non verbal signs as to whether you are getting what you want and just change your style or method.

## Rapport

A key part of what you are doing here is building rapport. This is not pretending to be someone's best friend and faking interest in something you are not interested in. It is trying to be sensitive so that the person you are talking to feels a sense of affinity and is prepared to talk to you even if you are in an adversarial position – watching out for their sensory system helps, matching breathing tonality and body posture in a subtle way will help.

Let us give you an example of this. You get a very angry customer on the phone. They start shouting "this is the second time your company has let me down". Conventional customer services wisdom insists that you quietly calm them down.

However first of all you have got to match their breathing and speech tonality otherwise it will make them more angry. I don't mean that you shout loudly at them, but you have got to match them to get rapport before you gradually level them to a solution. Try it and see. I found this out by an accident with an aggressive client who never seemed to respond to my calming measures. He found out my home number and rang me on a Friday night about a fairly minor problem. As usual he was sounding off. Unfortunately or fortunately as it turned out I answered his rather aggressive communication style in similar vein, simply because at 10 o'clock on a Friday night I could not be bothered to get into "calming down" mode. To my surprise I built a much more effective rapport with my client than before and that continues to this day.

The basis of rapport is that people communicate better with people who are like them. That does not mean that you pretend to like people you don't. However if you need a communication process to take place with anyone it is better to "be on the same wavelength". You need to show respect for how they communicate.

This can include their style of presentation, the words they use, non verbal clues, body language and even their cultural background.

Some people, quite often the successful ones, can do this effortlessly; you can do it too, and at least improve how you are doing, if you will start to practice rapport building.

*Exercise*

(a) Go into a pub or restaurant watch groups of friends and couples. Watch to see any signs of rapport
(b) Think of a difficult meeting you have coming up. Do a rapport plan with that person or group
(c) Practice building rapport on a daily basis. Be careful though you may become too popular!!

If you want to influence people you must build rapport before you attempt to influence/persuade. Otherwise lack of rapport will lead to a refusal to consider you point of view.

These skills need to be used with the best of intentions. If you use them you will suddenly find a whole new world opening to you, watch out though you may have too much fun!

**Networking**

The idea of deliberately meeting people socially with the prime purpose of advancing your career or business does not sit easily with some people. If it is done with the sole intention of using other people solely for your own ends, that is indeed shallow. However building contacts who will be of help to you can be a fun process and should be an ongoing part of your business and personal life. If you are totally antisocial and refuse to speak to anyone other than a few close friends, you may get some "browny points" – but unless you are either vastly wealthy or hold some position of power already accept the fact that you will be neither a business or social success. It is an old truism but one which you must take onboard "it is not always what you know but who you know".

We are trying to improve your personal influence to achieve results. I know in an ideal world these results should be based solely on your abilities and hard work. Sadly that is not the case. If you are really useless at your job or your business does not add value, your networks will not save you. However they do provide significant advantages to anyone who will work at networking on a continuous systematic way.

## Why are Networks so Useful?

Networks are firstly great fun, you will gain an understanding of a wide variety of areas. You will also learn a lot of informal information that would not reach you otherwise. You will also know a lot of people who know people who know people who could make a huge difference to the outcome of the project. There is something known as "the power of 6" which is the concept that everyone in the world is only six people removed from anyone else through the power of networking.

Your network through the power of geometric progression can reach out worldwide.

Let us say you have 5 key contacts they each have 5 and so on. Giving 5 levels $5 \times 5 \times 5 \times 5 \times 5 = 3125$ people. You can see the value of being "well networked" and how your "social capital" can be actually an asset. Of course it is not always the quantity of your contacts but the quality. It definitely makes a difference if you have some "key influencers".

Unfortunately what this means is that at business or social events people make a beeline for those who are perceived to be successful either in monetary terms or in terms of their "clout".

It works much better to be more relaxed and talk to everyone there. There is no point going if all you do is talk to the friends you came with.

Ironically the new people you meet, even if they are unlikely to directly present you with any business opportunity, will most certainly know someone who will. People pick up quickly on insincerity or those who will only talk to perceived "heavyhitters".

## Bad Networking

One of the worst examples of networking I came across was in USA. I was on an Entrepreneurship course and the evening was held to teach us how to network the American way.

The networkers either told us their life story or very quickly left us when they realised we could not provide venture capital or whatever their most significant requirement was.

The course leader was approached by a delegate, a medium ranking development officer whilst he was speaking to a senior ranking aerospace delegate. As he shook hands he actually looked away from the development officer and continued his conversation with the Aerospace "heavy hitter". This is the type of networking which turns people off. You are there to meet people. If you do not show sincerity or respect for them you will create the "negative networking syndrome". Bad news spreads twice as quickly as good news as the story above illustrates.

## How to Network

Always aim to meet at least two new people in any networking event. The natural thing which some people think after, meeting new contacts is "how can I use them to move my career/business forward". This "using" of people turns a lot of people off the concept of making new contacts.

However once you have met someone who you have found interesting, you should be "keeping in touch" and seeing if there is any way you can be of assistance to them". If you take this attitude you should be setting up a network of giving and receiving in an ethical way.

## Be Organised

The consequences of not being organised can counter the advantages of creating a strong network. You need to keep in touch with your network otherwise it dies. Making contact is only "half the battle", keeping in contact is very important. Set unambitious but achievable targets to keep in touch with your network.

Let me give you an example of how not to do it, again from my own repertoire. As a young ambitious consultant I was making contacts looking for key referral business. One enterprise agency manager in particular sent me 40 new clients in the first six months, a godsend for my business.

I really liked him and enjoyed spending time in his company. I became so busy that I never managed to see him for a year, feeling that having a cup of coffee with him was not "chargeable time". As a result I lost touch with a person I liked and respected. He also did not refer me any more business, not through any fall out, but because we were not in touch when he was referring a client. I was no longer the first name to spring to mind. A salutary lesson.

### Objectives

You should aim to meet at least three new people a week in connection with your business. Your job is to keep in touch with them on a planned basis.

## Networking Plan

For some of you, networking will come easily; some of you may already be blessed with a network through family contacts. However whatever the state of your network work at it.

The keys are:

1. network on an ongoing basis
2. keep in touch
3. try to help at least one person in your network every week

Silverman, a Marketing Guru in USA claims that networking is the number one marketing strategy for all companies. The reality is that your network will at times be the difference between success and failure in business. You have to find the right balance and go after it in a structured fashion. Set outcomes, review your performance at networking events, learn from great networkers. However do it in a relaxed fashion. You are meeting new people and connecting. If you are too focused on an immediate business return, people will feel used and the benefits both directly and indirectly will be significantly lower. Be sincere and continuously search for interesting ways to help and connect with your networks.

*Exercise*

Plan your next networking event. Send us a week's record of your networking activity with your own reflections to EFactor@aol.com. Lets Network!!

## SALES

### Introduction

The concept of selling is sadly an alien word to many people who want to be enterprising, start businesses or make projects happen.

Most people see selling as some type of socially unacceptable activity where people are sold something they don't want or need by someone who "cons" them into it. People spend their whole life avoiding this activity. However this need not be the case. As Robert Louis Stevenson said "everything is selling something all the time".

If selling means persuading someone to buy a product/service or idea, then everyone does do it. Any form of selling activity should follow on from market research and promotional activity. Trying to persuade someone to buy something they don't want or need is a waste of time and very inefficient.

However with a proper targeted audience you will have to persuade people to buy or support your project. You will need to sell yourself to your prospective boyfriend/girlfriend, his/her parents, prospective employer and a Bank Manager for money. The list is endless. Persuasive communication is of the key transferable skills you will need wherever you work in life.

If you decide to work in the Charitable sector you will need to persuade potential sponsors to back you, persuade your chosen target group to use the charity and influence volunteers to commit time and effort to the project.

So my basic premise is that everyone needs to go on a sales course. It is just we have all been programmed to hate that word. Don't mention the "s" word. It is ok to influence but not to sell.

I was attending a Management Development programme in London and was asked by one of the English participants as to what was my area of research and how I was applying the business model we were working on. I explained that I was applying it to sales. Unfortunately being of Northern Irish extraction I pronounce my vowels rather differently to someone from England. My new friend thought I was working with "seals" and was therefore a zoo keeper or circus performer. The conversation continued for 3 days until he asked me if I had worked with any other animals.

We eventually realised so much for communication that we had been talking about different things. However I sometimes do believe that people would rather work with "seals" rather than learn how to make "sales".

Learn the skills and use them appropriately and ethically. However I do believe much of what you achieve in life will be based on what deal you make with family friends and business associates. Until the other party agrees to back your proposal nothing happens. Persuade and influence in an ethical way or leave everything to chance. It is your choice.

## Selling is a Process

There are stages that any sales or influence situation goes through. So we will try to analyse each stage as it happens and advise use of what behaviours to adapt or learn.

### Stage 1 – Do Your Homework

It is important that you are trying to do a deal with the person who can make the decision or who could be potentially interested in talking to you.

Do market research and do not waste your time in targeting the wrong audience for your product or service. It is that attitude which gave selling a bad name which used to be prevalent in a lot of the sales industry, sell your product to anyone you can find whether they are interested or not. Persevering is a strong quality but hounding people who do not want to know is unethical and wastes a lot of time.

## Prospecting

So qualify your prospects. One of the key ways of keeping yourself dealing with only those who are potentially interested is to build in a steady flow of prospects that you can work with on a relaxed basis. You don't then have to "power hose" the one or two people you have found by chance and you can then concentrate on finding the right mix of person versus product or service to make the sale and achieve customer satisfaction.

*How Do You Prospect?*

Find out as much as possible about your potential customer. Let us say your ideal customer is a woman 25-35 with a child under 5 with a family income of £35000. Where do they live? What do they spend money on? Where do they shop?

You need to develop a system to make them aware of what you offer. You need to use a variety of low cost strategies to create enquiries.

Use six to seven different strategies. If they are targeted at an audience who clearly need the benefits of your products it will put a number of enquiries into your pipeline.

However the key thing is to do this on an ongoing basis so you never run out of potential customers or deals.

What most people do, be it someone starting a business or someone looking to get potential members to their new club is to stop prospecting the minute they think they have enough business or enquiries for their project.

It is better to continually work at it because converting interest into sales or deals will vary and you will need to play a numbers game.

A rule of thumb that sales people often follow is that you need ten enquiries to get an appointment and ten appointments to get a sale.

## Relax Not Everyone Will Buy

If there was one lesson you could learn from this section, it would be this. Not everyone will buy from you, even though market research has shown them to be an interested customer.

Yet many of us are sensitive souls at heart. If we talk to someone about our project and they do not give us a positive response, we take it personally.

I used to run a programme for women entrepreneurs. Many excellent graduates came on the course. They had good ideas, and worked hard at developing their business. Unfortunately when most of them tried to make their first sale they were devastated and a lot of their businesses did not go any further. It's a national pastime "Avoid Selling".

## Listen and Ask Questions

We have mentioned the importance of listening before but it is a key skill in persuading others. Listen to what they say and look for signs in their tonality or body language which indicate what their key area of concern is.

To get the right information ask questions to get their reaction. Ask open questions which allow the potential customer to show their true motivation. You are trying to find out what their "hot button" is, what matters most to them and trying to diagnose if you can provide a solutions with your product/services. The big moment which tests your integrity is when you have listened to the needs of the potential client and find that your business does not offer an appropriate solution to their needs. Are you prepared to walk away, even though you desperately need the sale?

The answer is you have got to be. If you want to build a relationship of trust with the customer you must act in their interests. Easy saying that I know. Play fair Today get rich tomorrow!

The answer is by developing more prospects, and having people continually going through the "pipeline" you can be more relaxed about who buys now.

## Dealing with Objections/Closing

Welcome objections, it gives you the chance to deal with any potential problems.

You have also got to be prepared to close. A classic example of someone not doing this was John Cleese playing the part of a sales rep who was calling in a stationery shop week after week and having cups of tea with the owner. A stranger appeared with forms to be signed and he then left after five minutes. John Cleese innocently asks "who is that", "Oh that's the man we buy our stationery from".

What was the message? John Cleese represented all those people who make contacts with potential prospects, build a relationship but never actually ask for the business.

If you want to achieve results with your selling/presentations, you will have to ask for the work/business. It is a nice idea to think that once you have made contact with the "customer" that they will offer you the business, However you need to ask for what you want. Sir Alan Sugar of "Apprentice" fame is very clear in advising would be Entrepreneurs that they need to clearly ask for what they want.

Part of the problem goes back to the fear of rejection. As part of the cultural bias against the concept of selling, some people will react rather inappropriately if they feel they are being sold to. You need to relax and realise that "some will some won't" so what next? Asking for the sale, yet being relaxed about the outcome is the key.

## Closes

Some professional sales people will learn a variety of closes in order to "trick" the customer into buying. You need to ask for the sale as part of the process and pick up on the signs where the customer still wants to buy and where he is wriggling out of it.

Like every negotiation the sale is only made when the contract is signed and money passes hands. It is vital to tie down the final details because it is the difference between getting the business or not.

Like all skills you will get better as you practice. Selling and personal influence are very similar and you ultimately are judged by the results you achieve. However you may learn more from the sales or negotiations you lose, than the ones you win. Take at least half an hour after every major "pitch" to assess what you did right or wrong. If you have been interviewed for a job you have the right to ask for feedback. Gradually you will get better. It is not always obvious what you have done wrong and you may need to rely on informal feedback and non verbal signs.

A friend of mine who was being interviewed for a job as a teenager shut the door on the head of the second interviewer when walking nervously into the room. He didn't get the job (what a surprise!!) It is not always as obvious but learn from your mistakes and you will get better.

## AIDA

As we said earlier sales is a process. It is important that you do things in the right order.

AIDA is a mnemonic for

Attention
Interest
Desire
Action

This is the normal process you need to stage manage before you have a chance to make the sale.

Following this process will gradually build interest and lead to the opportunity for a decision.

### A – Attention

Let's see how it works.

Whether doing a presentation at a job interview or doing a "pitch" you need to get the attention of the people you are dealing with. Hopefully if you have done your homework before the meeting you will have an idea of the best way to attract the attention of your audience. What you are searching for is their "hot button" what will attract their interest. For instance if you were trying to sell a product and you know the company's main focus is on cutting costs, an opening remark like, "This product will save you £15,000 per annum" is likely to get you at least a fair hearing.

### I – Interest

You need to get your audience interested.

Be clear and try to communicate in a meaningful way to attract and keep their interest.

Do everything possible to bring your presentation alive, use visuals, vary your voice – if it's a product have a sample.

Make sure your communications style is appropriate for your audience. If you are trying to "sell" community service to teenagers you need to talk their language and build rapport in your presentations.

Again being clear as to what you want to achieve is necessary. The excellent communicators will also be flexible and note if their audience are losing interest.

### D – Desire

Basically your audience will only want a solution if you can show that you can give them one of their main desires/benefits. By this stage you should have found out what they are and you need to show how you can meet these desires.

Equally if you can't genuinely meet one of the key desires/benefits, you should not pretend. Honesty at this stage will give you a strategic advantage with your potential customer in the long run.

### A – Action

If you have got your client interested and have shown how you can solve their problems, the key is to now ask for the sale to see if they are prepared to take action. If they say "let me think about it" that means they are not ready. It is important to read what the client is really thinking when they are looking for a way out and not wasting your time.

## Flexibility

Ultimately although you follow the same process, how you behave can depend on what you are selling and who you sell to.

It is good to have a process and organise each stage. However each company/person is different and it is important that you respect that difference. Some will need help in making a decision, some will not respond to any type of aggressive approach. Your ability to deal with a wide audience will depend on your competencies including belief, self confidence and ability to master your fears.

However the most important thing is to change your attitude to selling. It is a natural communication process and a vital life skill. If you are to achieve goals you must influence other people to support your cause provided you do it with integrity it can make the difference in whether a business deal is done, a community project is backed by funders or indeed whether a relationship is formed.

You have been learning a full range of enterprise skills. Basically an Entrepreneur finds an idea and makes it happen. To make any project happen you will need to convince a lot of people, suppliers, customers, banks and staff to support you and believe in your project. Your ability to influence them to support you will play a key role in the success or failure of the project. Influence or fail!

If you have very little of these skills and no network you may feel you are not in a position to influence what happens.

However start where you are now, decide what decisions you need influence with, set a plan and if you will complete the tasks set you will gradually improve your ability to influence customers. You can do it, if you will start practicing the skills in everyday life. It's up to you!!

## Tasks

1. You have been asked to sell a new student health drink which cures hangovers. Prepare a 3 minute pitch. Create a short written plan then actually make the pitch to friends/family – ask

for feedback. E-mail me with your written plan and reflections at efactor@aol.com

2. Look ahead over the next three months to where you need to persuade someone to back you. Create a sales plan. Practice delivering it. Then carry out the actual presentation – What did you learn? What can you do better?

3. List ten things you can improve to help your influencing skills

4. Try to meet 3 new people every week who are important to your business. Email efactor.com once a month to confirm you have done this.

5. Twice a week for the next month, find an opportunity to practice gain new skills. Email me, tell me what you have learned

6. I want to give £20,000 to the best sales pitch I receive in the next three months. Email me what is your idea? Why should I back you?

7. Practice persuasion skills every day. Let me know how you got on. If you still want to improve email me and I will give you my full list of suggestions.

Go on make my day, Persuade me!!

# — 7 —

# LEADERSHIP AND TEAM BUILDING

## LEADERSHIP AND TEAM BUILDING

You need to be a leader. Whatever project you are involved in you need to use all the resources including yourself to make it happen. This will include buildings and finance but above all people. Leadership is not management. You need to inspire teams to achieve the projects and be the best you can be. Leadership is your capacity to turn a vision into reality.

### Leaders are Congruent

To be a leader you need to have several of the E Factors as part of your behavioural make up. You need to be able to take action, to know what your customers are, understand business issues, have confidence and personal mastery, and the ability to influence others to follow your leadership and as a team make the project happen.

You will be better at some of the E Factors than others, but if you want your team to be innovative to personally develop and learn you need to set an example and show them that you are dedicated to the principles you are asking them to follow. In other words "walk your talk". Are you paying lip service to the ideas of the new project or are you dedicated and prepared to work along with your team.?

### Belief

Part of your goal as a leader is to have belief in your vision. Not only do you have to deal with your own doubts you must inspire others by the power of your belief to take action to achieve the vision. This belief should not waver at least in public until the project is achieved.

### Vision

You should have a clear strategic vision of where you want you and your team to end up. Can you see clearly the outcome of the project? Can you see it happening?, can you think strategically beyond where you are now? How do you get better at this? Practice visualising long term goals and the strategic aims of your organisation.

### Team Player

Ironically most of the time as a leader you need to be a team player. You may need to lead the team but you need to be integrated with it and be able to work within the dynamics of the business using the power of the team to realise your objectives.

### Inspire

You must inspire others to join your team, your company and to take action. Your belief will do that but you need to motivate others, give them belief that the project will happen. The ability to "sell" them on your business or company is also significant.

### Flexible

Flexibility is one of the key qualities of the enterpriser. You need to know when to inspire, when to allow the team to get on with it, and when you must intervene to deal with a major blockage. Although most theorists would now favour a team based leadership approach, your style of leadership may need to vary according to the type of organisation you are leading, the type of project and the type of people involved.

Many leaders tend to have one style which works for them 70% of the time. Can you vary your style when a situation or the people involved require something different.

Leadership is very much a communication process and in communication you need to follow the standard formula which I believe also applies to leadership. Know what you want. If you as a leader do not know where you want to end up, what chance does anyone else have? Take action and be able to measure whether you are getting the outcome you need at this stage. The ability to then change strategy of the first one is not working is the work of the good leader who knows the achievement of goals are not always completed in a stereotypical way.

## Delegate

As a leader although it is good to have an idea of what happens with the detail you cannot afford to get bogged down in day to day details. Leaders need to find others to deal with these while they focus on taking the business or company forward.

## Face the 20% that Cause the Problems

In running any business project there are many things to do. However there are certain key issues that are always likely to cause problems for instance confrontations with troublemakers, difficult decisions to make. You shouldn't delegate these, they are the responsibility of the leader! It is those key activities which will make a difference and where a leader will make their mark.

## The Ability to Think Perceptually

When you are making decisions regarding the future of your company, it is important to be able to see customer, staff and other stakeholder viewpoints. Your ability to gauge any changes in this is a responsibility of the leader.

## Break Things Down

As well as sharing the vision you need to be involved in the design of the shorter steps that will take you there and the obstacles that will get in your way.

## Find Managers Who are Better than You

If you are recruiting a team to take the business forward, look for people with special abilities. You may feel threatened by them but you need their expertise. Even if you are a small business start up with all the lack of resources that are implied, look for key staff or external advisers who have the capacity to help you realise the vision. To go to someone who is cheaper tends to be short term thinking.

## Look for Communications Opportunities

Find new and creative ways to make things happen.

## Rewards/Compensations

Give people a vested interest in the business to lock them in for the long term. Use short term celebration opportunities as flexible opportunities to reward people and show your appreciation in an unexpected way.

## Clear Up the Leadership/Management Distribution

It is your job to create values and design how the plan is going to work. You will need the help of management to execute. You also should make the decisions once you have sought expert advice. Your auditors or business consultants may give sound advice as to how to run the business but you as leader must decide and use them to help you make your decision which is the one that matters.

## Everything You Do Matters

You are as a leader setting the organisational culture. If you come in late, don't carry out promises or threats people at all stages of the organisation will act the same.

I have worked for organisations where the leader was very negative into micromanagement and tended to have similar people in positions of control. Needless to say that was not a very motivating environment. I have also worked for organisations where the leader had a vision that inspired you and made you want to be part of the team that brought about the impossible.

## Tough but Fair

I fully support the collaborative leadership model where achievements are very much the team effort. However there is a human trait where if you appear too "nice" that they feel they can "push your luck". If you have good information and communication systems you will hear through the "grapevine" where someone is doing this possibly carrying out activities which conflict with your mission. The danger of course is to overreact over small issues. However rest assured if for instance one of your managers has done something which you don't approve of it will quickly become a habit they will not stop, and you can end up with a much more significant problem.

## Leaders are Listeners/Readers

You should always be looking for information formal and informal and listening to feed back both external and internal.

## Leaders are Creative

Your ability to solve strategic problems creatively are important together with your reaction to the fast pace of innovation. You should be open to new ways of ding things because if you find the right innovation you can significantly change things for your business.

### Leaders Like to Learn

I am constantly amazed by the Leaders of growing and large companies who are keen to learn, build clusters and network with other Chief Executives. They may have achieved conventional success but they are constantly looking for one or two ideas often from competing industries that will make a difference in their own particular business.

## Coaching

I see coaching from two angles. Firstly as a leader who should be able to coach others to motivate them and provide the springboard for them to achieve high performance. Your job is to listen and facilitate the development of your key objectives.

The ironic thing is answering the question who coaches the coach?

As a leader you may be in a position where although there may be Boards of directors or shareholders who you report to there is no one acting as your mentor. You need someone not involved in the day to day decisions to help facilitate you in your decision making. Getting coaching is a worthwhile investment. You set out your goals and have someone as a sounding board to motivate, encourage and help you without being directly involved in your career.

## Respect Others Style

You should have the capacity to work with a variety of senior people with different styles. You need to work on your ability to create rapport with them all, and your capacity to create group rapport when you all meet together.

## Trust

Creating a climate of trust and integrity is your job. You need to gain the trust and respect rather than get it because of your position. How you behave will ultimately decide whether your team trusts you and will work with you.

*Task*

Are you a leader? What is your vision of your organisations future?

## Learn from Models

There are many people who have successfully created a transformation of organisations large and small, private and public. Read their books, network with them, watch what they do. Copy their behaviour that works.

## Values

It is up to you to impose the values from the top. Those values might include things such as customer service or integrity. You need to set them out that it is very clear that is how everyone must act.

## Your Personal Leadership Style

Are you clear what your personal leadership style is? How can you enrich? How can you improve? You should be looking to acquire the behavioural skills that will achieve the results of good leadership. Identify any weaknesses in your style. Can you unblock any competencies where you have been found wanting? Let us say you were a successful small business owner and you are now a senior leader in a public sector organisation. How have you adapted your behaviour to be the best leader you can be in that particular situation?

*Task*

Name a leader that you admire.

## Confidence

You need to be confident and well organised. You may not always feel confident about yourself or your business. However your influence is important on all the stakeholders. Your confidence will be infectious but so also will your obvious lack of confidence. Your style will influence what the organisation does.

You will also command respect to ensure feedback and action from your staff.

## How Do You Motivate Your Team?

You must make people feel part of a team, offer opportunity for advancement and to fulfil their ambitions within your organisation you need to take time to listen to key individuals and to watch their non verbal language together with their words to assess what is really important to them.

## State Management

Your ability to control your state and focus (see personal mastery) is important as particularly in times of crisis your team will look to you for the way forward. Your ability to appear calm, focused and in a powerful state will have a strong impact on how the organisation as a whole responds.

The ability to get your best performance when you want it is important. The challenge you may have is that you may only work at your best, when under stress, you need to be able to recreate this state at any time not just in a fire fighting crisis. The better your performance as leader at the strategic stage, the less fire fighting there will be.

### You Will Use Planning and Creative Models

Part of your job is to plan the future of your organisation. You need to have the capacity to see creative possibilities, allow others or yourself to suggest new ideas and then be able to disassociate yourself and take a critical view to iron out any practical difficulties.

### Overcome Limiting Beliefs

The key challenge will be to overcome the limiting beliefs of other key influencers in your organisation. You need to understand their perspective, respect it and find a way to gradually win them to your way of thinking. This may include achieving small targets building trust and belief step by step. The key is to get others to practice as if thinking even if they believe practically there is nothing can be done.

### The Right Message

We have mentioned what an important part communication plays in leadership. The worry is that other key players may get the wrong message. Miscommunication can be very difficult. You need to carefully consider the media used that it is appropriate to achieve the clarity that is needed. Communication and persuasion will play an important part in your leadership style.

### Learning

Your ability to lead the group is influenced by your own beliefs and functions. Being aware of this is half the battle. You also need to learn the level of charge required and the situational demands of your particular leadership situation. Something you will need your team to develop all the ideas, sometimes you will need to do a lot of stimulation.

*Particular Leadership Skills*

Research has revealed a lot of skills you can develop. It is not enough to know you should show strong belief. This is a behaviour/skill that you must work on to take to the level of unconscious competence, where through practice you appear to be a born leader. The skills can be divided up.

*Personal Mastery*

1. Establish a vision and a set of interim steps to implement that vision
2. Keep yourself your goals and personal states aligned to your mission
3. Practice building your belief to achieve your mission
4. Work on your flexibility in leadership style and ability to influence skills

*Working with Others*

Realise that people do think differently. You need to win over people who are against the changes you want and you need to overcome resistance to change by whatever methods work best in that situation. Your respect, ability to listen, build rapport and ability to put yourself in the position of those against the changes is a good start before you begin your campaign of influencing. Look at how styles work with people, the problems and the level of change.

*Skills Requirement*

You need to build your motivation and communicate to your highest level. You will need to work at times not only on your own tasks but on those you need to influence. Unless you match your mission with their values or get them to change their values you will face a strong resistance to change.

## Sporting Heroes

I realise that some of you will love sport and many of you will have no interest. However sporting leaders do behave in many of the ways we have outlined and for some are great role models. Stephen Gerrard Captain of Liverpool (a team I don't support). His team were losing 3-0 at half time in the final of the Champions League to AC Milan the hot favourites. Somehow himself and Rafael Benitez the manager turned things around. Benitez was very calm at half time. He did not speak of victory but of getting a goal back, a first step and changed tactics as clearly the initial strategy was not working. He also reminded the players to play to show their appreciation to the fans, all 42000 of them who had turned up at Istanbul and were singing the Liverpool anthem "you'll never walk alone" still after watching their team being humiliated in the first half – Benitez set the team the short term goal of scoring in the first ten minutes. When Gerrard their leader on the pitch responded with a fantastic goal, he used all his belief to motivate the rest of the team that they could do more. The rest is history. A wonderful example of belief flexibility action and leadership linked to great teamwork.

There are lots of examples of political leaders locally and abroad who have worked to a mission and made substantial progress in its achievement. However I think I will stay clear from naming examples. This book is controversial enough!! I also do believe you need to want to win the finish job. As a sign of leadership, Benitez the Liverpool manager is now getting rid of some of his squad who although they over performed in the final, but did not "do the business" on a consistent basis. This may seem ruthless but for a project to develop you will have to make tough decisions which will work strategically but may often be very unpopular short term. Some people find this impossible particularly if they have excellent rapport with their existing team. People need to be treated properly but the mission is everything and sacrifices have to be made. There are examples of leaders who have removed themselves from the chief executive role for the good of the organisation. Many entrepreneurs who have the leadership qualities to take a business from nothing to the growth stages may well want to leave the "stage" at plc stage when the company is listed on the stock market as they realise they are inappropriate leaders for a company in this environment where relations with "the city" and corporate governance regulations become much more significant.

## Ethics

If the leaders ethics are suspect, this can lead to the lack of ethics at all levels of the organisation. The ethical mindset of the leader should cascade down through an organisation.

## Clear Communication

Everyone you deal with should be clear what you expect of them.

## Promote Learning

You should encourage any staff to develop to be the best they can be. For some this may be scary a bit like bringing in highly talented individuals whose abilities you feel may surpass you. However bringing people in and looking for peak performance should be a value that will set your organisation apart.

## Decision Making

When the time comes you will have to make difficult decisions. How do you get good at decision making? Probably making bad decisions and learning from them. An appreciation of all the key business dynamics including marketing, finance and people are important as sometimes a leader who is a specialist in one of these areas will tend to make a decision which focuses on the aspects returning to their own discipline. For instance a leader with a marketing background might overlook strategic financial or people consequences in their decision.

## Energy

You need to have the energy to manage change and keep a project moving on. Hopefully you will have something left for your private life to maintain a work/life balance.

The ability to relax no matter what the circumstances is good not only so you can make detached unemotional decisions in times of crisis, but also because too much stress saps your energy and undermines your capacity to perform. Time spent with family or taking exercise will tend to be time well spent even from the business perspective.

However driving a project ahead in uncertain conditions can create an adrenalin rush which can be addictive. However when you see some of the high performers taking time off on a regular basis you may realise that energy, relaxation exercise and an outside life can be much better not only for you but also the business. Beware of being "busy" doing things that don't really make a difference to the end result. An hour wasted at the office is an hour you could have spent with your loved ones, or just enjoying life.

## Risk Taking Decisions

One of the key lessons is that you must be a risk taker to be a successful entrepreneur. Even in the public sector when you are put in charge of a new organisation such as the child support agency you are taking a risk to some degree.

There is some truth in this but not in the Gung-ho ideal of a ka-mikaze pilot who dives in not caring what the consequences are for anyone including him or herself. Any new enterprise is a step into uncertainty. The best business plan in the world cannot guarantee what is going to happen and even with the best laid plans you may well have to change direction and use all your innovative skills to respond and keep the organisation going.

What separates the entrepreneur starting up a small business from the manager of a new company subsidiary in a large organisation are the more serious implications for the individual if there is a corporate failure. Most small ventures are started with inadequate resources and often some capital from the funder. The owner will be personally liable for debts unless he operates under the protection of limited company status but even with that protection as he has ownership personally he is likely to lose more financially than the corporate new venture manager. He or she will at worst lose their job and any potential bonuses but provided the failure is not linked directly to their inadequacies may be moved to a different role within the company.

So yes a leader is a risk taker because they will often be instigating change and pursuing a strategic vision in an uncertain environment. However even the entrepreneur can limit their risk to be a calculated one. The problem often with your own venture and without control from a holding company is that you are allowed to take all the decisions no matter what your previous experience and often you lose the power of detachment. Your business can become an emotional attachment which many people hold on past its sell by date for ego or because they want to keep the business going for staff or the community even though the model no longer works. So yes you do need to be a risk taker though the type and extent of the risk varies from project to project. The better you plan and use the E Factor Skills the better your chance of success.

## A Good Leader Knows When to Go

A great skill can be to follow Kenny Rodgers advice in the song "The Gambler" "you got to know when to hold them, know when to fold them". Military leaders from time immemorial when they sensed the battle was definitely not going their way knew when to cut their losses to live to fight another day.

## Decisions Under Uncertainty

Managers can make decisions within definite operational structures. Leader operate under uncertainty you will have to develop the capacity to make decisions which is against popular opinion but that will strategically make sense. You need to see possibilities that others don't see.

You need to make decisions and be prepared to see an action plan up straight away.

## Learn from Your Mistakes

Sometimes you will call it wrong. A leader will take responsibility and be prepared to learn from the failure. A leader knows that failure will happen at least short term. The leader will learn and if need be change strategy or timescale to achieve the goal.

Ultimately you need to not just to drive your team to develop and be the best you can be. The hardest part at times is to manage yourself so you carry out your inspirational role. Sometimes you may feel as down as your team and have to hide it from them. Acting as if you believe will help, but always be yourself.

When I first went into business I had a set vision that a leader had to be loud, a great public speaker who aggressively motivated the team.

Having since observed many leaders, I notice there is a variety of styles. Some leaders will be quietly spoken support their key players and lead mainly by example. They are persuasive and will lead by bringing the team along and only take a different approach when there is a need for a change of strategy.

As the leader you set the agenda. You also set the culture of your organisation – whatever behaviour you expect your team to show, you must demonstrate on an ongoing basis.

Although there are eight factors in total, being enterprising involves identifying an innovation or opportunity and making it happen through your leadership skills. Sometimes there will not be a large team within the company, but even one person projects will be working with regional agencies, suppliers customers, Banks and business advisers. Your ability to lead them and make them all work towards the mission will make the project happen. Develop your own leadership style. Your main example may be someone who has operated in a different time, company or project. Learn from others but develop your own style based on your beliefs and strengths. Someone who can lead others need not have any particular technical knowledge but have the capacity to develop strategic vision and make it happen. Find opportunities to lead. Your ultimate potential will be realised when you develop as a leader create a new project and make it happen with a team, After that anything is possible.

### Task

In the next month find at least one opportunity to lead a project in business or the community. Make it a project that you are passionate about. Make it happen, learn along the way and above all have fun!

## Teams

You will have noticed that this chapter I write about both leadership and teams. In my view the two areas are linked. A team needs to be lead and a leader will only get his vision realised through an excellent team. Many people who go into entrepreneurship start off with the concept of doing it alone. However any enterprise will benefit from group work and from the synergy that a good team can provide.

### Team Development

Any team will take time to develop. There will be possible conflict as everyone finds their roles at the start and people often talk that the team goes through the process of development, storming norming and performing. That is why a clever leader needs to be there to coach, facilitate and cajole as the team performs.

One of the problems is that you will sometimes have someone on a team who does not want to be there. They should be given every chance to get into alignment with all other members of the team. However if this fails sometimes you have to consider an exit route if they are not adding something to the team.

## There is Room for Different Roles

Management development research has revealed that the ideal team will have a mix of individuals all with different strengths. The ideal would seem to have been everyone with very similar outlooks and skills but a mix up with a range of skills and outlooks will perform much better provided they can work as a team eventually. Most teams will need a leader facilitator a strong team player who will always focus on team togetherness, someone to raise alternative viewpoints and someone to persuade people to take action. The key is can all the individuals bring something to the team. Ultimately if as well as their own individual skills it would be great if everyone respected the team and wanted it to perform well.

The team whatever its healthy differences should all have the same mission on a strategic fashion. There has to be a compelling reason why they are together.

## The Purpose

Just as it is important for you to have a purpose, the group needs one. It is particularly vital at the early stage when there is some inevitable conflict and also at a later stage when a lot of the hard work has been done and the group cannot quite finish off the project. Why are you here? In many cases the why is more compelling than the how. I would suggest that you get your team together as early as possible and everyone has to answer the question "why am I here?"

The group will no doubt have conflicting purposes and ideas but you need to find a common purpose. Until the purpose of the project matches that of the group, it will encourage negativity.

It would be good if the group could get inspired or motivated at this stage. However grandiose motivational speeches have their place, but can too easily wear off.

At this stage the team also need to create their values, and to set a blue print as to how they will achieve the strategic goal.

A facilitator can be a great hope to resolve conflicts to drive the purpose agenda. The facilitator can also help to build the vision, to work on beliefs and to challenge any negative beliefs which start to surface.

### Develop

Everyone in the team should have an agreed PDP, personal development plan. Team activities should be arranged to encourage team building. Everyone should understand other roles other than their own. The use of reward and recognition to show that the team appreciates each individual will help.

### Team Power

Although you may be the leader of the project you want to use the power of the team. You should seek opportunities to allow others to show leadership. A series of team tasks will help to make the team believe they can get results together and build the sense of morale – Always be looking for the team and individuals to stretch a little further each time.

### Be Positive

Look to reward and recognise where anyone is acting for the food of the team or are actively developing new behaviours.

Have fun. A team that plays together works together. This should not be forced, but a systematic series of fun events will change the team make up.

I worked in one organisation where we all mainly worked as consultants on individual projects, when we had fun days or evenings out every event seemed to create a potential team spirit. The only problem there was a year between each event and we all went back to out own individual projects. Ironically most of us have now left the organisation and still get on well. What a waste of group potential that was.

*Task One*

Think of a team project you were involved in. How did the team function? What role did you play? Was this the most suitable role?

## Are You a Team Player or a Loner?

Many of you will start your own organisation because you want to run things your way. However you need other people when you start you might be operations, HR, marketing and Accounts – As you expand you must build a team around these specific functions.

You will find this difficult particularly if you have ignored the value of being a team player from the start. However much of the enterprise literature shows that the creation and building of the key team and a similar ethos within the company will play a strong role. However some of the most effective teambuilding activity I have seen done by entrepreneurs is where they manage to turn their Bank Manager, Accountant, Lawyer and Business Advisers into an informal seamless team which work together on each project. You may have initiated the project but can you listen to others and try to get the benefits of team synergy. Can you take on board the input of others or will you bulldoze them down.? Big Business is a team sport and you must learn the skills.

## People Skills

Can you give feedback to other team members? motivate and encourage them for the good of the team? Can you show and give trust and build rapport with other team members? A genuine interest in understanding the perspective of others is important. Honesty is vital but you need diplomacy particularly in the early stages to know how far you can go.

## Group Brainstorming

As soon as you can get together a group of people from diverse backgrounds. Ask them to come up with ideas for a new project. Prepare to be surprised how a group can come together how their different perspectives can lead to the creation of a wide variety of ideas.

## Have a Team Coach

It is useful to have someone not directly involved in the team to facilitate the group. Observation of how people perform in a group with individual feedback can help people adjust their behaviour. In many groups the key problem is someone who naturally dominates the group. This can demotivate other members from taking part. Hopefully the group will bring them into line, but at an early stage a facilitator might help.

### Task 2

Have a group meeting you attend videoed. Get someone to observe and let the group watch the video. Who is open to learning?

Some people such as entrepreneurs may be used to working on their own and must learn to respect the group and realise that their behaviour must adapt in a group.

## Original Individuals/Great???

Many people who individually do not contribute much, in the right group dynamic can make an effective contribution. It is all about getting to the Three Musketeers stage "one for all, all for one" attitude. People want to be valued and want to play their part.

I was recently involved in taking an enterprise course. A number of students were randomly assigned to a group and had to complete a number of tasks over the period of a week. My role was to facilitate the group. The group had everything, a very difficult individual who did not share the values of the rest of the group, a very strong minded dominant individual, some people lacking in confidence. My role was not to tell the group what to do but at times to ask questions to help self awareness. The group went through some very difficult patches early on particularly in regard to consensus decision making. Gradually the group took some shape, and the difficult individual and the dominant one both became more team players. Again it followed the standard procedure storm norm perform. The group found its own way to work. They were helped by having to complete a number of group tasks designed by the Belbin group, where physical tasks could only be completed by teamwork.

## Belbin

Belbin also have interesting psychometric tests to help provide information on how you perform in a group. What do you like to do in any team situation? The challenge is often if you have a number of excellent individuals who all want to lead there is likely to be conflict until a team consensus on leadership is found. An excellent lesson from the course was how important it is to be a team player. Many would be entrepreneurs take time to understand the concept. Equally the group has to guard against assuming the qualities of an ineffective committee. The group needs to find someone who will keep them on course, and not let it descend into a talking shop without any service of goals or mission.

### Task

Set up a small team to generate business ideas. Meet once a month for three months. Work to build a team. What did you learn? Would you have had more ideas as an individual?

### The Ski Trip

It does take time to form a group. Many entrepreneurs will keep bringing people in and then replace them immediately trying to find the right individuals. The ideal is to give a new team a series of achievable tasks and as momentum built up really go for it. On a recent ski trip I was able to observe and learn a lot about group activity. We were a variety of school parents thrown together for the trip. We were all beginners and all lacked confidence. As we went through the difficult early stages of learning to move on skis and then tackle the more daunting tasks the ski activity was full of lessons for teamwork. Some of us who were falling less than others initially became impatient with others who were taking longer to learn the skill. One individual admittedly quite fit, moved himself up a group to intermediate after the first day so high did he rate his performance. We did not miss his arrogant attitude to the less talented skiers.

As well as learning individual ski skills the instructor focused on developing us as a group for a specific reason. We would eventually be going into tougher conditions in uncertain weather, and he knew if anything went wrong we needed to stick together as a group.

He did take it to extremes. As I lost control of my skis and was heading down the slope out of control he advised "stay with the group David". Everyone thought it was hilarious and needless to say I got the lesson. Gary a bit of a daredevil who kept heading off in an opposite direction to the group was constantly asked "where are you going Gary?"

I had great difficulty with the ski lifts particularly with the two main ones where you and your partner needed to stay balanced to keep it moving. However at the end of the week we all as a group completed the ladies Olympic downhill. Those of us who were trying to individually excel had learnt that supporting the group and having respect for everyone whatever their athletic ability was more important than our own ego. The beer was good too! More team building!

## Conclusion

You need to learn to lead enterprises but also be a team player. This applies not only to colleagues within your company but to a lot of external stakeholders. Collaborative relationships will ultimately prove much more successful if you have a "win win" approach. Learn to be a team player lead from the front and watch that project happen!

*Task*

List the teams you work with. List 3 things you can do to build the team/collaborative framework.

# 8

# OUTCOME/FLEXIBLE ACTION ORIENTATION

## OUTCOME/FLEXIBLE ACTION ORIENTATION

You need to be outcome orientated, that is constantly know what you are looking for strategically as well as here and now. However without the capability to take action on an ongoing basis you are unlikely to achieve any of your outcomes. Outcome/action orientation is a key enterprise competency and needs to be backed up by flexible behavioural patterns. Once you know what you want you need to take action. However there are likely to be changes or reactions which may get in the way of achieving your targets. Your ability to notice feedback, verbal, written and more informal methods that tell you what result you are getting is key. If you are not getting the result required you may need to adopt a different strategy until you get the results you need.

This may seem obvious but you often find the sorts of individuals in the enterprise world who push very hard but get mediocre results at best because they do not observe the above rules. People who when they have an idea in their heads immediately go for it and take action without any thought to consequences or regarding what they actually want. This is better than no action at all, but is almost a "scattergun" approach one step forward and then one step back. You also get individuals who once they have devised a strategy act on it and will keep on doing so regardless of the consequences. The effect is a bit like keeping banging your head on a wall hoping it will break. I know it may depend on how hard your head is and how soft the wall is the fact remains this is probably not very effective.

Why do they do this? Well if you are a disciple of positive thinking you will have developed a churchillian response "never give up – never ever give up" Determination and persistence are valued qualities in someone starting an enterprise and rightly so. However there may be a need to vary the strategy when it is not producing the results you thought.

Sometimes you may also need to review your outcomes when something changes in your business model or the environment which means that the original outcome is no longer valid. However outcome orientation is being clear about what you want at macro and micro levels. If you are unclear as to what you want and where you are going to go, the environment will reflect back your uncertainty and produce mixed results.

## Know What You Want

What do you want? Or as The Spice Girls said (sorry!) "tell me what you want, what you really really want". It is not always easy to know what you want particularly at a strategic level. You can get too busy passing exams, making a living and just getting by. Even worse you can often go into careers/relationships or even business agreements which are really based on someone else's wish list. A friend may ask us to go into business with them or your father may have always wanted to be a Doctor and now wishes the same for you. That does not mean you go for either option, unless it suits you. You can be vulnerable to other people's ideas. If you do not know what you want, either have your own plan or be part of someone else's.

### How Do You Know What You Want?

You need to take some time out. It is good to start off with some "possibility thinking" If there were no limits what would you like to do, how much money would you like to earn? What contribution do you want to make? Assume you have no limits.

*Task 1*

Take 5 minutes, write down as fast as you can without stopping anything you want to do or have in the next five years.

*Task 2*

Look at your list, pick one long term and one short term goal. How much do you want them? Why do you want them? Write these goals out once a day.

## The Most Vital Skill

You can see that knowing what you want is not as straightforward as you think, yet it is vital because you are setting out the direction of your life. Know where you are going and be able to measure it. There is very little limit to what you can achieve provided you have absolute clarity as to what you want. It is important that you know where you want to end up long term as well as short term to make sure you are on the right path.

Many goal setting specialists suggest thinking where you want to be in ten years time. If you can visualise this, then work back until now to see the in between steps. Try it now.

## Your Purpose

Life can change at any time. Your goals may vary but it is useful if you consider having a mission statement. A mission statement sets out clearly what you want to do to contribute to make a difference. This may sound a little prosaic but it is taking the view that you have a purpose to use your talents and abilities to help others. It is something to come back to if you are ever sidetracked which can easily happen.

Your purpose will usually include doing what you love and what you are good at – If possible try to put your mission statement into one statement.

For example let's say you enjoy coaching business people advising and encouraging them to be successful.

Your mission statement could be "I want to inspire and motivate business people to perform at their best". Everything you do in life should be related to that mission.

## The Why

It is important that your mission really motivates you and gives you a reason for taking action. You should be passionate about it otherwise it is not your mission statement. People are often familiar with company mission statements often framed and sitting in the reception area of a major company. The problem is that these are often someone else's mission that you may not agree with.

## Setting Out Your Mission

### Name Two of Your Talents

What are you good at and also really enjoy? Let us say you are an excellent teacher and you are very enthusiastic.

### How Do You Enjoy Using These Skills?

When have you used the above qualities? Let us say you have been the most enthusiastic when you have been teaching young children how to play Tennis. They loved your approach, were making progress and really enjoying your lesson.

*Set Your Purpose*

It would seem obvious that your purpose should be to teach tennis to kids. What we don't know is if there are other areas you would like to share with people. My suggestion would be that your mission statement would include sports coaching but go wider to include the general role of teaching.

"My mission is to teach others to be the best they can be using my enthusiasm and people skills. I teach business people and sports people of all ages to reach their potential and have fun"

It is clear why you are here, what you are good at. You may use various ways to harness that talent to help others but everything you do should be geared to teaching and working with people as it is clear that is what you love and what you are good at. When your purpose has these two qualities it is much more likely that you will stick at it and make a bigger contribution.

## What Do You Want to Be?

Once you have sorted out the broad principle, it is now time to be more specific. You will need courage to state this, because it will seem as if the world makes decisions as to what you should do. Parents friends workmates all will have pigeonholes they want to slot you in, perhaps partly for your own good (in their eyes) but also to achieve some goal of their own, sometimes one they are not consciously aware of.

## Work on the Want List Again

Spend another ten minutes writing down everything you want. You might start off with a list of material possessions such as a Castle, a maserati Etc, but somewhere in the list you may show what is important to you, what contribution you would like.

For instance let us say that when you go through your list, you find that sports is everything to you. It is the environment you want to be around.

The careers adviser would probably at this stage say fine that's your hobby now what work can you do to pay for that hobby?

However if you want to work in sports and you are an unlikely candidate to becoming a professional athlete, there are lots of other options available.

1. Sports agent
2. Sports coach
3. Sports lawyer
4. Physio
5. Sports finance
6. Run a leisure and sports complex
7. Become a sports journalist
8. Come up with a new product which could be used in your favourite sport
9. Sell sporting autographs
10. Become a sports psychologist

You can link your skills and enthusiasms to the area you love.

## Where are You Now?

People often find it hard to realise where they are now compared to their end vision. It is important to self assess and if need be get feedback from those around you. Don't fool yourself, there is no other place you can start, than where you are now.

## Your Vision

Try to build a picture of your future. Visualise your job, career or business. What is your income? What type of people do you work with? What exercise do you take? The bigger the vision, the more you will believe it.

Spend ten minutes everyday going through that vision in the same detail.

It is important to know strategically what you want because if you don't know where you are going in the long run it is very easy to go off course. As Tony Robbins a renowned motivational speaker put it "in ten years time you may not know what you want, but you will surely arrive!" It can seem like a waste of time to think ten years ahead but actually like Robbins has suggested while you are making up your mind about where you want to end up, you can wake up and realise ten years have passed.

Strategic goals can change but it is likely that your life purpose will always be with you. You may demonstrate or use it with different groups or situations, but the true essential you and your talents will be there. It is important when drawing up your long term vision as to where your talents will take you. For instance a teacher who wants to share his/her subject with the world and be a successful business person may think "that is not how education works, education is done within the public sector; a high level principal or administrative post must be my aim" however I noticed the vision of Robert Kiyasaki founder of the "rich dad/poor dad" brand which teaches financial literacy. Robert is a teacher at heart but has created an online community which plays a game he uses to teach the principles of financial literacy. He also has a variety of information products which educate and conducts seminar tours, simply because he refused to limit his vision.

## The Power of Goal Setting

You have no doubt read many times about the power of goal setting. Basically if you have goals it tends to give you more direction and a greater chance of success. You need a list of goals short and long term, for most aspects of your life. For instance if your only goal was to have your own business by age 35, earning £150,000 per year, the danger is that if that is all you focus on it may be the only thing you achieve and find yourself with no personal or social life as a consequence simply because you did not set goals in this area. This pleases the army of negative thinkers who use the lonely success story as an example of why it is better not to have goals. However where goal setters, set targets in both their business and personal life, they can have success but not at any price, and a proper work life balance.

## Do You Need to Pay a Price?

Depending on your goal there is a price to pay. I don't believe it has to be your social or family life. However you do have to remove a lot of things from your life that do conflict with your goals.

You need not take on too many outside projects that could conflict with the aim. However the power of goals is in setting out measurable targets that can measure your progress on the road to achieving your vision/life purpose.

## Features and Goals

Goals should be positive, specific and measurable. For instance if you say "I would like to give up smoking in the near future" you are not following a couple of these conditions.

Firstly your goal is negative there is no specific timescale set to target the outcome. This is not a goal, but a vague aim which of course is going to be much more difficult to achieve.

### What Will I See, Hear and Feel to Know I Have Achieved My Goal?

This is looking for the sensory evidence that will tell you, you have achieved things.

*What Will I Lose?*

It is important to consider what benefits you are getting from the behaviour you want to change. When you are setting goals it can be useful to question why you want it. For instance you say you want a 7 series BMW a good question to ask yourself would be "why do I want it". You may genuinely love German cars and really want this model but if you find as you do on some occasions that you want to be respected and admired because you drive a BMW Series 7, it is the feeling you want more than the actual item and it might be better to work on getting that feeling met.

*Write Your Goals in Detail*

Spell out the detail of each goal as this is important for visualisation, for your subconscious mind to accept it and start finding opportunities to make things happen.

## Level of Goals

You need goals that will stretch out but are still achievable. If your main goal is to have lunch in a restaurant two days this month this is very achievable but will not stretch you at all. However if you want to become president of the USA by Friday that is pushing things too far. However one of the key benefits of setting a goal, and then working towards it, is your personal development and what you will learn on your journey towards achieving it.

*Key Goal*

What one goal could have an impact on all aspects of your life? which goal would be life changing? Goal setting should not be a one off thing. It is something you do for the rest of your life. You should certainly have more than one.

## Obstacles

There will be obstacles put in front of the goals, some within yourself such as a specific fear or obstacles provided by the outside world. What can be good is to anticipate and plan for them and welcome them. Obstacles are part of the process and you will deal with them on your way to achieving your targets. Ideally you want to find out as soon as possible what they are, and face them.

As we have noted not only do you want to achieve the goal, but you should ask yourself "what type of person do I have to become to achieve that goal".?

That is why people who achieve against obstacles and have to stretch to achieve a goal have a greater advantage over someone who achieves the same goal by luck. If you become a millionaire by business and financial strategies you will have developed a skill set which you can turn to again and again. Whereas if you become a millionaire by wining the lottery, ironically it is another lottery whether you will hold on to the money and prosper as the wealth is not a result of a process of actions and skill development.

## One Step at a Time

How do you eat an elephant? One bite at a time. Once you have set goals and I recommend 5 year/1 year, quarterly, weekly and daily goals it is the actions you carry out that will achieve the results – sometimes there will be an opportunity to have one significant breakthrough but usually it is step by step.

## What Resources Do You Have?

It is useful to identify what resources are needed to achieve the goals and whether you have them now. Do you know the right people? Do you have money? What do you have going for you to help you attain your goals and what do you need to get?

*Task*

Set out your goals for 5 years. Pick one in work, personal development and personal life.

Do the same for yearly, quarterly, weekly and daily. Do your goals pass the test? Do you really want them? Keep a mini goals book and three times a day look at your goals list.

## Review

Review both your goals and your performance on a regular basis. Do you still want the same things? Are you on target? What should you do differently in order to achieve your strategy?

## Outcome/Thinking

You need your own personal goals and try where possible that these goals do not conflict with your business or work. You do need to consider the ecology of the situation. Is there any area of life which making your goals happen which could be adversely impacted.? For instance if you have a young family and your goal is to travel and work abroad 28 days per month this is unlikely to leave a lot of time for your family and will cause pressures/conflicts. That is why it is important to discuss your goals with the people in your life. Their support or not will play a major part.

## Outcome/Orientation

In order to be more effective you should always have an outcome orientation that is whatever you do, you should have thought ahead as to what result you want and acted accordingly. Let us say you get on the phone to speak to a prospective customer it is important that you are clear about what you want from the call. You do not want or expect to make a sale over the phone, what you want is to make an appointment for a face to face presentation. Therefore you must ensure you do not try to sell your product/service too much over the phone and lose sight of your goal.

If you go to a networking event what do you want to achieve.? If you go and stay with your best friend the whole evening you have failed Much better to have reviewed the guest list and set yourself a realistic target to meet four new people to include two people who could be customers for your company.

Thinking even for a moment about what you want to achieve tends to focus your mind on the key things and makes it less likely that you will waste time and lose focus on what should be the possible outcome. Meetings are famous for people getting drawn into discussions about irrelevant issues and things going off on a tangent. Hopefully if there is a chairman it is their responsibility to keep to an agenda, however it is up to you as an individual to have your own outcome focus to ensure you get what you want to achieve from attendance.

The same principles apply

- What positive outcome do you want?
- When specifically?
- How will you know you have achieved it?
- What resources do you need to gather?
- When will you review it?

There is a strong correlation between being results orientated and taking action. Focusing on outcomes is a 20/80 activity that will increase the likelihood of you taking appropriate action.

You may get a little worried where you will be seen as one of those people who "always has an angle". Where people, particularly in your personal life will resent where every seemingly innocent conversation or action has a purpose or hidden agenda. You do need to switch off at times, but to maintain work/life balance the enterprising person needs to be making things happen and therefore does particularly in business not want to waste valuable opportunities that will be presented at conferences business meetings or negotiations.

## Action Overrated

I find it is really hard to know when the outcome setting ends and the action begins and vice versa. This is because outcome setting without action is a complete waste of time, but similarly doing things for the sake of it is equally so. I am sure you have heard the quote that a definition of insanity is doing the same thing over and over again achieving the same result.

Focused action is the key but outcomes and action are part of that seamless loop we discussed earlier where outcomes are set, action taken, feedback monitored and action taken possibly of a different nature to keep driving to the initial outcomes.

There is no doubt that we are discussing the second key feature of Enterprising behaviour. We have talked about being creative curious and innovative to identify opportunities. Action is the other feature in the equation. Sadly a lot of people do not take action even when a golden opportunity is present. Why? Let's discuss this.

## Why Do People Not Take Action?

Firstly as stated it is difficult without goals or outcomes to take any appropriate action. However there are a whole host of other reasons. Many of which have been discussed in detail in this book.

1. Belief

   Lack of belief will mean you will feel that whatever you do will not work.

2. Personal Mastery

   Lack of confidence and negative emotions such as fear of rejection or failure will also be inhibiting factors.

3. Assertion

   People will lack assertion skills to state what they want and take action.

   By working on these "E Factor" skills you will increase your chances of taking action. It is always easy to get negative habits such as procrastination and that is why it is recommended that once you have set a goal, you take a first small step towards the goal.

4. Desire

   You may think you want the goal you have stated. Many people when asked to state a goal say they want to be a millionaire. If presented with a process or blueprint to achieve this goal most will say yes they would like the money but not enough to be prepared to go outside their comfort zone. Taking action and being proactive usually involves getting out of that zone and many people are just not prepared to do this unless they are pushed.

*Task*

What do you want to change in your life? Are you prepared to do something about it? Face Facts

## Inability to Think Strategically

Many of us are a bit like pavlovs rats. Provided we receive immediate reward or reinforcement on taking action we are keen to do so. You must realise that there are some steps to take that will make a difference in the long run. There are often activities which are important but not urgent but which will have an impact in the long run.

**"Paralysis Analysis"**

Many highly educated people, academics and professionals will be capable of analysing all the problems of a new project and in dissecting an opportunity. The problem is the more you do this, the more you can identify the challenges and the uncertainties. However new projects/opportunities will always have uncertainties and part of the core skill of the enterprising person is that once they have done their homework and overall feel comfortable with the calculated risk they will go for it!

Northern Ireland where I come from has one of the best Enterprise support networks in the UK but also one of the lowest rate of start ups particularly amongst women. We also have one of the best educational systems in UK. Invest NI the local regional development agency has had to go so far as to spend significant funding on a promotional campaign urging the population as a whole to "go for it". By providing road shows, role model etc they hope to change the culture by making people aware of all the help they need.

However much more focus is needed on improving action orientation for individuals. I feel that too much education and training for entrepreneurs is awareness training and the provision of information. I personally feel action learning should play a bigger part and that students or trainers should actually do things and practice the behaviour skills outlined within this book is much more likely to lead to the start of a new project rather than information on the tax system and analysing a case study. Ironically many of the people who lead the courses have never actually started a new enterprise successfully or not and are therefore advising others to go for something they haven't done themselves. They will try to bring role models in which help but ultimately enterprise action needs to be taught or mentored by people who have very direct real life experience to share.

**The Inner and Outer Enemy**

Your inner critic will be one of your toughest opponents. You need to learn to override the fears that hold you back. Actually it is that first or second step, no matter how small that will help to lead to further action. There is also jealousy in a lot of us if we see someone doing something we would not dare to do, instead of encouraging them and admiring them for their willingness to take action, there is almost a collective commitment to knock them for it and secretly hope that it doesn't work for them to justify our own position.

So you can see there are lots of reasons why people don't take action. It is a lot easier to talk about doing something or even to show somebody else how to do it how rather than to do it ourselves.

### So How Do We Turn You into Action Man/Woman?

As you can see we can analyse why people don't take action and infinitum. This is missing the point as people will often find a new excuse to show why they never get round to things.

As someone who is actively involved in encouraging people to come up with business ideas they never seize to amaze me. I have proved time and again that creativity is a learned skill and have been amazed by the quality of the ideas provided by the participants on my courses. It is not part of my remit to cajole them into turning the idea into reality but I think it is time I moved into this area. So many of them having come up with the idea, can barely consider even protecting the Intellectual property. One group of participants last November devised a new piece of equipment for the hospitality business. I then noticed the idea identified as a great opportunity in The Sunday Times Business supplement. I went to see the group the next day, get yourself down to the patent office explaining how highly the idea was rated. "may be after our exams in February". Was the reply. Needless to say it never happened. It does not make this group of participants, bad people. In fact they were very nice. For whatever reason they represent the silent majority. All capable of coming up with great ideas/innovations but somehow never getting round to doing anything.

## The Steps

So what should you do to become more action orientated?

1. The first thing I want you to do is every time you have a new idea. Do something no matter how small a step it is you want to start a new project buy a book on it – make a call.

2. Get a coach! A coach is not someone who advises you. They are someone who helps you plan your own action plan and then do everything in their power to make you carry it out. They will ring, email, meet, inspire/push. Sometimes a paidCoach is the answer. Your boss, bank manager boyfriend/girlfriend family may be too involved to be detached. You may be lucky to have a role model who does this for you as a friend. Getting a coach even for a short time will boost your capability of taking action.

3. Keep your word – From now on only agree to do something for somebody if you are 100% committed. If there is any uncertainty as to your commitment then say no. What you are doing is training yourself to keep your word to yourself. So that you understand when you say yes you will do something it is as good as done. This means a lot to customers, financiers etc and ensures your action orientation.

4. Chunk it down – break things into small manageable tasks and start doing it now.

5. Persist – Take action be relaxed about the outcome. Obstacles will appear, stop draw breath, take action again and find a way round the obstacle.

6. Reward – Build your why up to increase self motivation. If you need to do something you don't want to, give yourself a small immediate reward for taking action.

7. Find what drives you – If you are doing this for your family, remind yourself at least once a day why you are taking action now.

8. Start today – Remember there is no tomorrow. Ask yourself every day, what action have I taken towards my goals?

9.  Always keep your plan goals to hand – Look at them every-day at least once. You may only have five minutes free in the middle of all the fire fighting. Use it for something no matter how simple.

10. Get any form of support or help you can.

11. Work on your personal mastery – how do you see things, do you see the project happening? Are you visualising it happen-ing every day?

12. Seek out a like minded person and support each other.

13. Time Management – Leave time to take some action every-day and keep a journal.

14. Have weekly review sessions with yourself to monitor the process.

15. Learn Self Discipline – Practice self discipline. Even if you want to start on your diet or daily exercise or the, something you were never going to get round to do. For instance let's take exercise. Start off with 5 minutes simple exercise every day. Doesn't seem much but every day you must make time for it. Build up gradually to fifteen minutes every day. Not only will this help your health and energy but again you are playing games with the subconscious mind. You are showing it that you can have self discipline and make yourself do something every day. Whether you want to or not. It doesn't matter what the focus is, it is literally that you are practising self discipline. Some of you may have this quality already. For the rest of us it is the unpleasant part of turning any idea into a reality. Constantly attack your comfort zones if you are do-ing something which is an easy routine, find something different to do.

16. Task – List 3 comfort zones you have. Attack one of them.

17. Adopt a motto/affirmation – Use something like "just do it" get yourself a paradigm that works for you "I will take ac-tion" "I will make it happen", "action is the key". I was inspired to write this book and have done so in less than a month after reading Jeffrey Archers Prison journals. Strange you may say, but it was the fact that despite the harsh prison

regime Jeffrey Archer made himself get up at 5 O'clock every morning to write for two hours. Of all the traits self discipline is the one you must master. It is related to motivation but where self discipline kicks in is when the motivation to do something is not there at present but you still do what you have to do anyhow.

18. Find Motivational Aids – there may be a movie or a sporting event which motivates you, a piece of music. I am rather partial to anything that reminds me of" Rocky". If you have got to take action, maybe do something which includes a confrontation you would rather avoid. Remembering a role model who was able to confront a big problem. What would they do? How would they act?

19. Act Confident – You may feel less than confident. However moving confidently and acting confidently will not only give a confident stance to the outside world but also will help you to take action.

20. Find your own motivation strategy. It may be you only really get moving when you are facing imminent disaster. You need to then visualise all the dire consequences you will face if you do not take action. Sometimes people wait until external circumstances push too far so they will take action. Create the circumstances yourself.

21. Keep an action journal – At the start of every day – ask yourself "What three things will I do today to move my life forward?" At the end of everyday record faithfully whether you did anything or not.

22. Only get interested in profound knowledge, that is knowledge that you can apply to your everyday life. If you are studying Business strategy or attending a seminar on innovation, ask yourself what one idea from this lecture can I go and use now?

23. People always say that information is power. However information is only of any use if action is taken. If you sincerely want to develop your enterprise capability you are in fact on a mission to improve your ability to take action, otherwise known as personal power. Knowledge of a skill is

known as personal power. Knowledge of a skill is no use because it is not part of your normal behaviour. The only way to do this is start practising every day. Having a do it now attitude is good. You need to work on your E Factors Daily – Practice the skills until they are part of you without thinking. To me there is nothing more cruel than having knowledge or opportunity but a lifetime of inaction means you let the opportunity slip by.

24. Work on your state – To get into the action frame of mind – Usually you will feel empowered, in the right state, with belief you can do it now.

25. Model the people who take action – What is it about their beliefs, their thoughts and physiology that you could copy? Look at world leaders but also look at successful local entrepreneurs or community leaders.

26. Be Congruent – Make sure your voice, tonality, posture all match up.

27. You need energy. At times you will have limited opportunity to take the action you need. If you are tired or run down you will find it so physically difficult to do what you know you should. Sensible diet, sleep and exercise patterns will help together with working at relaxation so that stress will drain less of your energy away.

28. Listen to William Shakespeare in The Merchant of Venice "If to do were as easy as to know what were good to do chapels would be churches and poor men's cottages princes palaces" Where you are now in life is a direct result of all the action you have taken to date. The chances are that if you take the same action you will end up getting the same results. You need to realise that you may not always feel positive but continue to take positive action. Performing an act of random kindness can help. If someone is struggling with a trolley help them.

29. Limit your actions to the key 20% that make the difference. Don't waste your action muscles on unnecessary activity. Only take action where you can have an impact.

30. Take action on one area of your life at a time – that area that is bothering you most. Find the key breakthrough things you must do and concentrate on them. Draw a schedule showing aim, action sequence and action start date.

31. Don't waste time get into action. Every day you contemplate is a day wasted. Research and analysis is useful but you will learn from action things happen, some good some bad if you can be flexible in your response you can then take more appropriate action. The momentum you create will open up opportunities for you. Time is your greatest resource, every day you do not take focused action is a day wasted. The most successful entrepreneurs I have met were not necessarily workaholics. They used their time well. During 9-5 they took action they took the actions where they made the most impact. They then enjoyed their private lives after that.

What three actions could you take now that could have the most leverage in your life? Do them today not tomorrow. As is often said, anyone can do it, they can if they will set their outcomes what they want from life at a macro and micro level and take focused action, respond where the desired result is not being immediately achieved and do something different if it will achieve a result. A great Enterprise person will have the personal power to take action when it is necessary. Like a tiger on the prowl they will seem relaxed watching what is happening however when the timing is right they will put all their energy into positive focused attention.

Do it now! Don't delay. Always plan ahead look for what you want then act on it, roll with the punches and keep taking action until your goals are achieved. Go for it!

## Conclusion

So we have reached the end or is it the beginning?

I hope you realise that you can be more enterprising and improve your "E Factor" wherever you are now.

There are a few key things you must do to take the ideas you have looked at here and apply them to your life

1.  Visit out website www.efactor.com and do our E Factor assessment tests
2.  Decide which of the E Competencies you need to work on
3.  Do something today!
4.  Pick 2 ideas to work on
5.  Constantly search for opportunities to apply these, keep a journal and learn
6.  Email us once a month

### Remember I Am Your E Coach

If you could just take one idea from each chapter and make it part of your life. You could make a massive change. Let us help, work on your key efactors. And see the change in your world. You were born to be Enterprising. It is time to do something about it. Do it now!!

# BIBLIOGRAPHY

1. Buzan Tony "Creativity" Wiley

2. Covey Stephen "Seven habits of highly effective people" Simon and Schuster

3. De Bono "Lateral thinking" Penguin Books

4. Kennedy Gavin "Everything is negotiable" Arrow

5. Kiyosaki Robert "Rich dad poor dad" Warner

6. Ryan Dave Marshall "The streetwise guide to starting your own business"

7. Senge Peter "The fifth discipline" Doubleday

8. Silverman, D "Word of mouth marketing" Simon and Schuster

9. Sugar Sir Alan "The apprentice" BBC Books

10. Thompson Geoff "The great escape" Summerfield

11. Trump Donald "The art of the deal" Wiley

12. Wilde Stuart "The trick to money is having some" Hay